What the Eagle Sees

INDIGENOUS STORIES OF REBELLION AND RENEWAL

ELDON YELLOWHORN & KATHY LOWINGER

 annick press
toronto + berkeley

Cover art/design by Tania Craan
Edited by Chandra Wohleber
Designed by Tania Craan
Photo research: Mac/Cap Permissions

To Jasper and Giovanni—EY

My grateful thanks to Rivka Cranley, Chandra Wohleber, and DoEun Kwan, as well as all the staff at Annick Press who have made this book possible, and to Bill Harnum for his many careful readings of the text. —KL

With special thanks to Nadine McSpadden, Secwepemc, Indigenous educator, Surrey School District, Surrey, British Columbia, for her detailed review and suggestions.

We acknowledge the support of the Canada Council for the Arts and the Ontario Arts Council, and the participation of the Government of Canada/la participation du gouvernement du Canada for our publishing activities.

 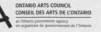

Library and Archives Canada Cataloguing in Publication

Title: What the eagle sees : Indigenous stories of rebellion and renewal / Eldon Yellowhorn and
  Kathy Lowinger.
Names: Yellowhorn, Eldon, 1956- author. | Lowinger, Kathy, author.
Identifiers: Canadiana (print) 20190066334 | Canadiana (ebook) 20190066342 | ISBN 9781773213293
  (hardcover) | ISBN 9781773213286 (softcover) | ISBN 9781773213323 (PDF) | ISBN 9781773213309
  (EPUB)
Subjects: LCSH: Indigenous peoples—North America—History—Juvenile literature. | LCSH: Indigenous
  peoples—North America—Juvenile literature. | LCSH: Indigenous peoples—North America—Social
  conditions—Juvenile literature. | LCSH: Indigenous peoples—North America—Social life and customs—
  Juvenile literature. | CSH: Native peoples—Canada—History—Juvenile literature. | Native peoples—
  Canada—Juvenile literature. | Native peoples—Canada—Social conditions—Juvenile literature. |
  Native peoples—Canada—Social life and customs—Juvenile literature.
Classification: LCC E77.4 .Y45 2019 | DDC j970.004/97—dc23

Published in the U.S.A. by Annick Press (U.S.) Ltd.
Distributed in Canada by University of Toronto Press.
Distributed in the U.S.A. by Publishers Group West.

Printed in China

annickpress.com
Also available as an e-book. Please visit annickpress.com/ebooks for more details.

CONTENTS

· · · · · · · · · · · · · · · ·

Author's Note

What the Eagle Sees tells the story of what Indigenous people did when invaders arrived in our homelands. I don't try to tell the whole vast story, and in places I don't tell it in the order it happened. What you will find here are some of the places and people and events that have mattered to me in understanding my people's past.

A word about names. I use the word *Indigenous* to refer to the people I am writing about. In the past, names like Indian, Native, First Nations, and Aboriginal were in use. Where they are still being used, like Indian Relay, I have kept the names intact.

For hundreds of years after the Europeans' invasion, Mexico, the United States, and Canada did not exist, but I use those and other modern place names where they will make the text easier to understand. I say Turtle Island to refer to North America, as do many North American Indigenous people for whom, historically, the North American continent was the whole world; they adopted the name Turtle Island from the myth that their world was created on Turtle's back. Finally, I have tried to use individuals' Indigenous names whenever possible.

EAGLE'S
TALE

If we listen, every bird and animal has a story to tell us. Of all the birds and animals, Eagle tells the most important story of all: the story of life.

Eagle flies over everything, so he sees everything: he sees daylight and darkness, summer and winter, dry land and water, snowy mountains and cool valleys. He sees beauty and ugliness, war and peace. He soars so high that he is the go-between between humans and the Chief of the Sky World.

Eagle has the gift of flight and a freedom that we humans can only dream of. Maybe that's why we tell so many stories about him, stories in which Eagle is the king of birds, or a chief who talks with humans, or a sage advisor whose insights teach us life lessons.

Eagle inspires us to go where he goes, to reach beyond our grasp. That is why John Bennett Herrington of the Chickasaw Nation, the first Indigenous astronaut, took an eagle feather into space with him on the space shuttle *Endeavour* in 2002.

A Piikani eagle trap, or *ipsstsstsii*, in the Porcupine Hills, Alberta. Because eagles are such powerful medicine creatures, there are many restrictions against hunting or killing them. A person who eats even a bite of eagle meat is said to change into a monster. On the Great Plains, anybody who wanted an eagle feather had to pluck it from a live bird, so Indigenous Peoples devised special eagle traps. In the Southeast, only hunters expert in eagle medicine could kill an eagle. In my own Piikani tradition, eagles were caught and killed only for traditional purposes.

Eagle's feathers are part light and part dark. The history in this book is like an eagle's feather. Past centuries have been full of terrible, tragic events for Indigenous people. That's the dark side of our story. The light, hopeful side is that against all odds we have survived. If you want to understand the past, keep Eagle's ways in mind. Take the long view, like Eagle does.

Artists carve images of Eagle on totem poles, talking sticks, and other kinds of art, including pottery and jewelry. Zuni carvers in the Southwest make stone Eagle amulets for protection or healing.

NEVER EAT
AN EAGLE!

The English fur trader, mapmaker, and explorer David Thompson (1770–1857) was traveling to Lake Athabasca with two Cree men. They had not eaten anything in several days. In desperation, Thompson shot and killed an eagle. One man refused to eat any of it because he had heard that anybody who eats an eagle will become a monster. He went hungry that night. Thompson and his other companion did not become monsters, but a few hours later they were racked with awful nausea and stomach cramps. The man who had gone without his dinner reminded his companions that there is a good reason nobody should eat an eagle.

THE STORY
OF THE
OLD NORTH TRAIL

10,000 years ago to the present

SURVIVAL LESSONS

The Old North Trail is one of the oldest and longest roads in the world. A segment of the Old North Trail runs through the Piikani Nation where I grew up. It crosses the Oldman River just below Head-Smashed-In Buffalo Jump in southern Alberta. I have walked on the Old North Trail, jogged on it, and pedaled my mountain bike in its ruts.

My ancestors walked the trail in ancient times. Walking its 3,200 kilometers (2,000 miles), from the barren lands of the far north all the way to southern deserts and home again, took at least four years.

They followed physical landmarks, such as the Swan's Bill just north of Banff, Alberta, and Chief Mountain in northern Montana, along the east side of the "Backbone of the World," which we now call the Rocky Mountains. Some of them were on spiritual journeys. Others just longed to see the country or river or forest beyond the next hill.

Most of those who followed the Old North Trail were traders. The heavy sacks slung from tumplines—or straps—around their foreheads were packed with dried meat and tanned animal pelts to trade for razor-sharp tools made of a volcanic glass called obsidian or for precious shells to adorn themselves with.

An engraving from the 1700s showing Nootka Chief Maguinna, who controlled the fur trade in Nootka Sound, trading with Chief Callicum. Traded goods lie at their feet.

The Old North Trail

This Shawnee village on the banks of the Ohio River is one of the many different ways people lived on Turtle Island.

The Old North Trail asked a lot of every traveler. You had to be nimble because it ran across stony riverbeds and around buttes so high you could barely see the top. You had to know how to read the wind and the sun and the stars. Your only map was the one in your head that you created from your own past travels or the stories you heard from other travelers. You had to know how to respect other people's ways, because you would be crossing the territory of one nation after another. You had to know how to communicate, even when you met somebody who spoke a different language.

MUCH OF THE OLD NORTH TRAIL is gone now, covered in grass or concrete, but trade routes like it once crisscrossed the continent. Indigenous people knew broad horizons—there were so many trade routes that it's possible every nation included at least one person who had seen either the Atlantic Ocean or the Pacific Ocean.

The trails of Turtle Island linked people who lived in many different ways. Some lived in cities. Others lived in tiny hamlets surrounded by farmland, or in homes they carried with them. Some were ruled by royalty, while their neighbors might follow a chief and make decisions as a group. All of them had their own healers and artists, athletes and architects, hunters and farmers.

Despite all their differences, the many peoples had a lot in common. The Old North Trail and other trade routes like it taught my ancestors that understanding and knowing the land was vital to safe travels. Since the different groups who used the trails often had no common spoken language, they devised a sign language that let them communicate and forge ties with one another. They understood the importance of learning from the Elders who had walked the trail before them.

I remember the Old North Trail when I think about the invasion of our land: the lessons we learned from the trail would help us survive the hard times to come.

HOW DO WE KNOW?

Follow That Obsidian!

Archaeologists are detectives. The objects and cultural belongings they find are clues to mysteries of the past. For instance, obsidian is a volcanic glass that was very valuable because it can be shaped into razor-sharp tools. Archaeologists dug up pieces of obsidian in the two-thousand-year-old burial mound of a chieftain along the Ohio River. They knew that obsidian didn't occur naturally there; it must have come from over 1,600 kilometers (1,000 miles) away, in what is now Yellowstone National Park. How did the obsidian get from Yellowstone to the Ohio River? Did somebody travel west to get it, or did traders bring it with them when they traveled a thousand miles east? By looking at the distance between where such objects are found and where they originally came from, scientists can begin to unravel mysteries about how people traded and traveled long ago.

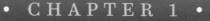

FIRST COME THE VIKINGS

WE FIGHT THEM OFF

982 CE to ca. 1400 CE

We've found a land of fine resources,
though we'll hardly enjoy much of them.

—Thorvald, son of Erik the Red,
Norse explorer, writing about events from 970 CE to 1030 CE

THE FIRST INVADERS
SKRAELINGS VS. VIKINGS

First contact! Fans of science fiction know this phrase well because the story that follows is told in novels, television shows, movies, and video games. Such stories usually begin with the threat created by aliens arriving on earth. The aliens have advanced technology and sinister plans. They try to enslave or destroy humans and lay claim to our planet. People seeing aliens for the first time react with fear and surprise. Then they overcome their shock and organize a resistance. They outwit the alien beings despite the aliens' superior technology. The happy ending always shows humans emerging victorious. For the Indigenous Peoples of the Americas, first contact is more than a virtual reality experience. It is a historical fact. We are still living with its results.

How would you react if you heard the news that beings from another world had reached our planet? What language would they speak? How would we communicate? What if you had to speak for humanity? What would you say?

There are ten of you, all hunters. You have been drawn by the smell of roasting meat and the smoke rising from a camp-fire. You hope that you will find fellow hunters who will give you a warm wel-come. But you have stumbled on a group of strangers with white skin and blue eyes. They draw their knives and clubs. Soon the ground is stained with blood. Nine of your hunting party lie dead, mas-sacred. You manage to escape to warn the others in your family. The news spreads among your people. They follow you back to the invaders, armed with bows and arrows, to fight this new enemy.

In the ancient *Saga of the Greenlanders*, a Norse writer describes how a war-rior's arrow killed the Norse leader Thorvald. Thorvald pulled the arrow from his intestines, saying, "We've found a land of fine resources, though we'll hardly enjoy much of them."

THE FIRST CONTACT between Indigenous people and Europeans probably happened more than a thousand years ago, when two very different groups of people met on the craggy coast of Greenland.

From the west came the Thule, the ancestors of modern-day Inuit. They left their homes on the shores of what is now called Alaska and within a few centuries they had spread across the north, all the way to Greenland and Newfoundland.

Inhabitants from Greenland around 1820

From Europe on the east came Norsemen, or Vikings. The word *Vikingar* means "raiders" in Old Norse. Vikings had a reputation all over Europe for being fearsome raiders.

The Vikings referred to the people they met in Newfoundland and Greenland as "Skraelings." It wasn't a compliment. *Skraeling* means "little men" or "barbarians" in the Old Norse language. As far as the Vikings were concerned, they had found riches: furs, walrus ivory, and fish. They intended to stay. Surely the Skraelings would be no match for Vikings who had made all of Europe tremble.

But as it turned out, in battle, the Skraelings were so fierce and unyielding that the Vikings were convinced to pack up and go home. At L'Anse aux Meadows in Newfoundland, all that is left of the Vikings' settlement are ninety-nine broken iron nails, a single whole iron nail, a bronze pin, a glass pin, and a knitting needle. Even their earthen houses have crumbled away to small mounds of dirt.

The Vikings had come to settle, but by around 1340, they had left Turtle Island. The first invasion by Europeans ended with them being driven back across the sea.

A historic Inuit house from the Thule culture made out of whale bones at Resolute Bay, Nunavut

THULE TECHNOLOGY

The Vikings might have lasted longer in North America if they had adapted Thule technology. No wood to burn for heat or light because there are so few trees? Burn whale and seal blubber for fuel and light instead. No wood for boat building? Stretch sealskin over driftwood frames to build kayaks and umiaks big enough to take to sea to hunt whales.

Kayaks are just one example of great Thule innovation. They are individually customized to the paddler's size, weight, and arm strength. A kayak is actually "worn" by its owner, who uses a double-bladed paddle. Its deck above the seat attaches to his or her parka, making a barrier against ice-cold water that might splash on the paddler and flood the inside. The deck is packed with a harpoon shaft, with a spear thrower extending from the grip end, and a harpoon head. Sealskin bladders act as drags once animals are harpooned.

THE VIKING LEGACY
STORIES THAT SHAPED OUR HISTORY

The Vikings didn't have any military or technological advantage over the Indigenous Peoples in Greenland or Newfoundland, and they didn't carry any new deadly diseases to North America, so these first invaders did not bring about the end of one world and the beginning of another. Life went on for the Thule much as it had before, except for the stories they told of light-skinned, hairy strangers.

AN ARCTIC MYSTERY

Who Were the Tuniit?

When the Thule and the Vikings met in Greenland, the land wasn't empty. The Tuniit people lived there. They are still a mystery. Archaeologists (who refer to the Tuniit as Paleo-Eskimos) think that they left Alaska on foot, about five thousand years ago. A thousand years later, they spanned the Arctic from the Bering Strait to Greenland. We know the Tuniit lived in Newfoundland from archaeological evidence: Their largest cemetery was found at a site near the town of Port au Choix on the west coast of the Great Northern Peninsula. Their favorite quarry for making stone bowls was at a site in Fleur de Lys on the east coast of the island.

The relics left behind by the Tuniit give us clues about how they lived. We know they had dogs but no sleds. They hunted from the edge of the ice because they had no boats. They built inuksuit, or stone people, as markers when they were hunting caribou. They built stone fish weirs to catch arctic char. They built houses with whale ribs covered with tents made of muskox hide.

Tuniit people don't exist anymore, except for the few traces they left behind, but they live on in stories the Inuit still tell—tales of timid, easily frightened giants who were so strong they could crush a walrus's neck with one arm and carry the massive animal home.

We don't know why the Tuniit disappeared shortly after the Thule and the Vikings met. Were they killed by invaders from the east or west, or did they simply blend in with the newcomer Thule people? We may never know.

Inuit artist Abraham Anghik Ruben (born 1951) grew up in Paulatuk in Canada's Northwest Territories, where his father was a hunter and his mother was a seamstress. His work has been displayed in galleries and museums around the world. In his sculptures, he explores the lore that Norse and Inuit cultures share as Arctic people, such as a belief in shamanism, a reverence for the land, and a common history of the sea voyages that brought the Thule and the Vikings together.

The Vikings abandoned their colonies in North America around 1340. When they returned home, they told their stories about sailing to the faraway countries they called Vinland and Greenland. They shared these sagas for generations before someone wrote them down.

What the Vikings wrote about the fertile land of grassy meadows and rivers teeming with salmon that lay across the ocean likely inspired more tales. Many people in Europe already had heard tales of seven cities of gold that stood on an island called Antillia in the middle of the Atlantic Ocean. Shipwrecked sailors had brought home tales of a mountain of silver. Some believed there was a fountain running with water that would grant eternal life to anybody who drank from it.

Rumors of those riches convinced Christopher Columbus and his peers to go out and find them.

Quetzalcoatl was a deity-king, kind-hearted (he didn't believe in human sacrifice) and wise (he was said to have invented the Aztec calendar, books, and writing). The people's affection for Quetzalcoatl made the rival gods jealous. They acted together to trick him. One day the Evil One went into Quetzalcoatl's palace holding a mirror. It was a false mirror. When Quetzalcoatl looked in it, instead of his own reflection, he saw a bearded, long-faced person. He knew that if his people saw him like that, they would be terrified. He had no choice but to leave. He went down to the seashore with his servants and made a raft of serpents. He told his servants that he would leave them, too. The servants wept, but Quetzalcoatl told them not to grieve. He promised that one day he would return and be their king again. Then he sailed away in the direction of the rising sun.

In March 1519, the Aztec king Moctezuma II heard news of bearded men who had arrived by sea from the east. He believed that Quetzalcoatl's promise had been fulfilled and that the god had come back. Instead of preparing his people to defend themselves, Moctezuma welcomed the Spaniards. When the Spaniards saw the Aztecs' elaborate buildings and beautiful jewelry, they believed that they had found the city of gold.

What resulted was a fatal misunderstanding. The powerful Aztecs could have defeated these light-skinned invaders, but they didn't because they believed their beloved god had returned. As for the Spaniards, their dreams of treasure seemed to have come true, and they believed that those treasures belonged to them, not to the Aztecs.

THE VIKING INCURSION had not changed daily life for the people of Turtle Island, but this new invasion was different. The Spaniards kidnapped and killed Moctezuma, and soon the Aztec empire fell. That was just the beginning of the violence and bloodshed that would affect Indigenous lives for centuries to come.

CHAPTER 2

SLAVERY

REBELLION

After 1492

We shall take you and your wives and your children,
and shall make slaves of them . . .
—The Spanish Requirement of 1513

SLAVERY ON TURTLE ISLAND

> ## imagine
> ▶▶▶
>
> The cry has gone up. Spanish slave ships have landed in the night! The sailors are torching your thatched homes. Resist, and you will be killed on the spot. Try to escape? Their dogs will track you down and maul you. You are herded into a holding pen on the beach to be shipped off and sold into slavery.
>
> There are three or four hundred captives on the ship. When it arrives on another Caribbean island, or in Europe, half its human cargo will be dead. You've spent days beneath the deck in the hold of the Spanish ship, lying in your own vomit and feces, and you are still alive knowing your fate is enslavement.

Christopher Columbus landed on the island of Hispaniola in the Caribbean in 1492 looking for riches to send home. The first riches he loaded onto his ships were the human beings he planned to auction off in the slave markets of Europe.

INVISIBLE
I N V A D E R S

Along with guns and a religious way of thinking that didn't allow for any other view of the world, Columbus and those who followed him brought deadly germs to Turtle Island. When Columbus landed on Hispaniola, there were about 125,000 Taíno living there. By 1535, there were none. They were all either slaves or dead from disease.

At the time, nobody in the world knew about germs and the diseases they caused. The plague, flu, measles, and smallpox were new diseases to North and South America, so people had no immunities against them. Beginning in the Caribbean, Mexico, and Peru, Indigenous people began to die from epidemic diseases brought by the Spaniards. The traditional medicines that cured so many other diseases were no match for these invisible invaders. More Indigenous people died from diseases in the first fifty years after the Spanish came than would be born in the next four hundred years.

Slavery has been practiced all over the world at one time or another. Turtle Island was no stranger to slavery. In the northeastern forests, the Haudenosaunee waged "mourning wars" on neighboring groups, taking slaves to avenge and replace their dead. Among the Kwakwaka'wakw of the Pacific Northwest Coast, raiders who captured nobles to make them slaves returned them if a ransom was paid. When Blackfoot warriors killed a foe in combat, they would take his scalp to send his spirit to be a slave of their ancestors in the spirit world.

Ferdinand II, King of Spain

The rules about slavery were laid out in the Spanish Requirement of 1513 ("The Requirement"), a document the Spanish were supposed to read to every Indigenous group they found.

The scene sounds ridiculous, but it was deadly serious. When they marched into a settlement, the Spanish invaders, sweating in their heavy armor and elaborate clothes, were under orders to gather the whole community together.

One of the Spaniards would hold up a piece of parchment and read out words in Spanish, a language that meant nothing to the baffled crowd.

The Requirement, written in 1513, demanded that Indigenous people recognize any king or queen of Spain and the pope as their rulers, or: "We shall make war against you in all ways and manners that we can, and shall subject you to the yoke . . . we shall take you and your women and your children, and shall make slaves of them . . . and we protest that the deaths and losses which shall accrue from this are your fault."

The deaths and losses came, though the fault did not lie with Indigenous people. Thereafter millions of Indigenous people were enslaved and sold in the Americas from the late fifteenth century through the mid-nineteenth century. In North America, the Indigenous population fell by more than half.

THE NEW LAWS

Spain passed the New Laws, banning slavery, in 1542. They were specific about the work that would be forbidden. For instance, slaves could no longer be made to do the agonizing work of diving as deep as 15 meters (50 feet) underwater several times a day on Mexico's "pearl coast" to find pearls to decorate the clothing of Spanish nobles.

The New Laws were well-meaning, but no one wanted to enforce them, and slavery continued to be practiced for hundreds of years.

SILVER
Tears of the Moon

The Aztecs called silver the "tears of the moon." People in Mexico treasured silver and had been mining it for centuries for themselves, in small quantities.

The Spanish invaders needed silver to make the coins that were to become the first international money. Slaves in Mexico mined, produced, and processed 44.2 million kilograms (48,722 tons) of silver.

Mining for silver was grueling work. Silver is buried deep in the ground. Getting to it required a shaft longer than 122 meters (400 feet), dug with only heavy picks and crowbars. Think about lifting just one pick, much less swinging it in the dusty blackness from morning to night. Then imagine swinging that pick while you carry a leather sack full of rocks weighing up to 113 kilograms (250 pounds). Now imagine carrying that load while you crawl through narrow tunnels or climb up a creaky ladder made of narrow pine boughs.

Slaves often fell or were crushed when tunnel walls caved in, or they died slowly from the dust that clogged their lungs.

REVOLT!

After the conquest, the Spanish took over the Aztec silver mines and expanded them. They looked north to New Mexico to find enough slaves to do the work. Forced silver mining was just one of the ways that the Spanish invaders made life intolerable for the Pueblo people who lived there. It was one of the reasons the Pueblos made a bold plan to end their oppression.

The Pueblo world was made up of some seventy communities called pueblos, each with its own customs and beliefs and language, spread out along the Rio Grande Basin through more than 483 kilometers (300 miles) of spectacular mountainous terrain.

Few Spaniards lived in New Mexico then—probably about three thousand—but they were armed with guns. A thousand lived in the city of Santa Fe near the central government building. That building, the *casa reales*, was so strongly built that it could withstand a siege. The rest lived in small settlements.

In the spring of 1680, the Pueblos of New Mexico planned to free themselves from the Spanish. They agreed that each pueblo would revolt on the same day to overthrow the invaders, burn down their churches, and unmake all Christian baptisms and weddings. By working together, they could erase every trace of the Spanish.

The plan would only work if the Spanish were taken by surprise, so secrecy was of utmost importance. Each pueblo had a medicine society that organized the town's ceremonial life. Only members of the medicine societies knew how to conduct the all-important rituals, so they were experts at keeping secrets. In total secrecy, all through the spring and summer of 1680, the societies met inside underground ceremonial centers, called kivas, to plan the revolt.

Taos Pueblo, established around 1250, is the oldest continuously occupied town in North America. The houses are built of earthen bricks or adobe. Units are stacked on top of each other, up to five stories high. Residents got to their homes by climbing a series of steps and ladders. People still live in the traditional houses today. Taos Pueblo is now a UNESCO World Heritage Site.

A fifty-year-old man named Po'pay became the leader of the revolt. Po'pay had personal reasons for hating the Spanish. Not long before, he had been one of forty-seven men the Spanish had accused of having supernatural powers. They accused Po'pay of carrying out the devil's work. Several of the men captured along with Po'pay were hung. One committed suicide. The rest were lashed or sold into slavery. Po'pay was one of the "lucky" ones. After he was lashed, he was released. He went home to Taos Pueblo eager for revenge.

The date for the uprising was set for the full moon of August, after the corn had ripened. In late July or early August, Po'pay sent out the runners with the news. It was the only way to communicate with the other pueblos.

The runners were astonishing athletes. Taos Pueblo is 113 kilometers (70 miles) from Santa Fe. To go from Taos to Isleta, the pueblo that was farthest

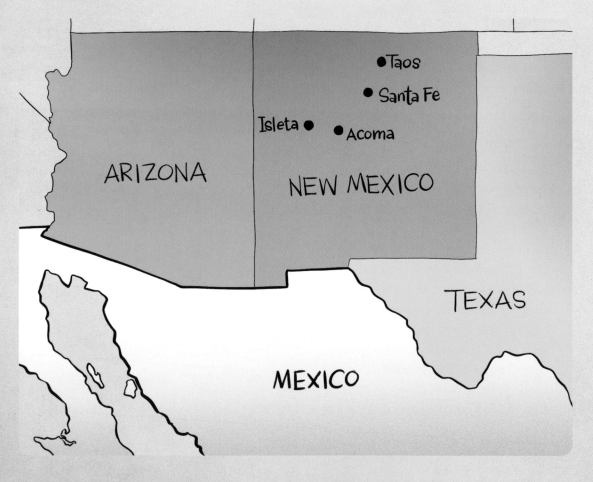

south, the runners would have to run 225 kilometers (140 miles)—that's like running five marathons in a row—in the scorching summer heat. To get to the pueblo of Acoma, located on top of a mesa, they would have to run 290 kilometers (180 miles), or seven marathons. And to reach the Hopi people, they had to cover 483 kilometers (300 miles), or twelve back-to-back marathons!

In pairs, the runners skirted mountains and followed rocky paths in canyon bottoms under the brutal sun. They had memorized everything about the plan, but they carried a bit of insurance: a cord of yucca fiber tied with as many knots as there were days before the uprising. Each pueblo would untie one of the knots to show that they would take part in the revolt.

Only a few days were left before the full moon. There were only two knots left to go. Then—it looked like the revolt was over before it had begun.

In the heat of the summer, the runners had to cross canyons and mesas.

The leaders of three of the pueblos dropped out. How could they possibly succeed against armed soldiers on horseback? Besides, every past uprising had failed. One uprising in 1650 had ended with nine leaders being hanged and many others sold as slaves.

Not only did the three pueblos want out of the rebellion, but their leaders traveled to Santa Fe to warn the Spanish about the plot. On top of that betrayal, they even told the Spanish where two of the runners were. Nicolas Catua and Pedro Omtua were still running with the cord.

The Spanish governor ordered the arrest of the runners. When Catua and Omtua were brought to him, they broke down and gave away the plan. The governor acted fast. He made sure that the Spanish in Santa Fe had firearms, he posted soldiers in the main church, and he stocked the *casa reales* with food and water so that Spaniards taking shelter there could survive a siege.

When Po'pay heard that the plan had been exposed, he didn't give up. He sent out more runners with a new message: "Don't wait for the full moon. We strike tomorrow."

Though they were many miles apart, on August 10, the pueblos acted as one, destroying Spanish houses, ranches, and churches. Some four hundred Spanish men, women, and children were killed. Po'pay rode from pueblo to pueblo telling the people that they should return to their old ways. The pueblos waded into the rivers so that they could wash away the Christian baptisms that had been forced on them.

In Santa Fe, the Spanish residents crowded into the *casa reales* for safety. The small building must have been hellish in the sweltering heat with a thousand men, women, and children packed into it.

Five days after the rebellion started, a Pueblo chief called Juan appeared in the plaza in front of the *casa reales* wearing war clothes. Indigenous people were forbidden to ride, yet Juan sat boldly astride a horse. Pueblos were banned from having Spanish weapons, yet Juan carried a heavy Spanish gun, a sword, and a dagger. Juan delivered the Pueblos' demands to the governor: all the Pueblo slaves were to be released, including his own wife and children.

A RUNNING
TRADITION

Indigenous Peoples have a rich history of long-distance running, from the Arctic peoples all the way south to those in Mexico, and across South America, too. Horses had disappeared from Turtle Island in the Ice Age, so until the Spanish reintroduced them in the 1500s, the only way to send a message fast was with a long-distance runner.

The list of famous Indigenous runners is long: 1912 Olympian Andrew Sockalexis (Penobscot Nation) would run down deer for his hunter father; 1909 World Professional Marathon Champion Tom Longboat (Onondaga Nation) from the Six Nations could beat horses in races of more than 3.2 kilometers (2 miles); and Billy Mills (Oglala Lakota Nation) won the gold medal in the 10,000 meter (6.2 mile) race at the 1964 Olympics. Today, many Indigenous high school students are involved in long-distance running.

Tom Longboat (far right) at a sports exhibition in New York City in 1913

Members of the Hopi High School boys' cross-country team head down a trail near Polacca, Arizona. Hopi High School has earned 23 state cross-country titles in a row, a sign of the enduring spirit of Hopi culture where running is rooted in this nation's tradition.

TOYPURINA'S REVOLT

Toypurina (1760–1799) was nine years old when the Spanish settlers first invaded the Los Angeles Basin of what is now California. As an adult, she became a respected spiritual leader in the Tongva Nation. Her people viewed the Spanish priests as evil shamans and held them responsible for the disease and misfortune they were suffering. Thus, the killing of a priest—an evil shaman in Toypurina's eyes—was a way to cleanse the land of spiritual evil. In 1785, Toypurina convinced the people from six villages to revolt against the San Gabriel Mission. At her trial, Toypurina bravely spoke out against the Spanish for destroying her people's land. Most of her followers were sentenced to twenty lashes, and Toypurina was expelled from her community and sent to live in what is now northern California, far from her home.

The governor refused to give in. As each day passed, the stench and heat in the *casa reales* got worse. The Spanish knew that the people inside would die of thirst, hunger, heat, or attack. At last, on August 21, 1680, they surrendered. They staggered out of the *casa reales* into the bright sun and set out for the south. The Pueblos could have killed them all, but they let them escape.

For the Hopi, descendants of the rebels who took part in the Pueblo Revolt, runners still bring blessings for the rain, for the harvest, and for a long life.

THE PUEBLOS could have killed the fleeing Spanish, but they did not. The Pueblo Revolt had succeeded. Over the following centuries, it would inspire Indigenous people to fight back against harsh treatment.

Although the Spanish returned to New Mexico twelve years later, the Pueblo Revolt is still remembered as an incredible story of leadership, cooperation, and bravery.

CHAPTER 3

OLD NATIONS CRUMBLE

WE FORGE NEW ONES

1592 to the present

A single twig breaks, but the bundle of twigs is strong.

—Tecumseh (Shawnee, 1768–1813)

STANDING TOGETHER

Slavery and disease almost wiped out the Indigenous Peoples of North America. Imagining the destruction is almost impossible: 90 percent of the population died. Nation after nation disappeared. The survivors had to find ways to replace them. And they had to do it fast, if they were going to stand up against European invaders. The stories of Deganawidah the Peacemaker, Wahunsunacock, Tecumseh, and the Red Sticks tell us about just four of the very different confederacies that formed on Turtle Island.

imagine

Most of the people you love have died from a terrible sickness. If they survived the long days of fever, painful sores covered their bodies. Somehow you survived, but you are left with pockmarks. Still, you are more fortunate than those who lived but were left blinded.

Hardly anyone remembers the ways to keep the good spirits close and the bad spirits away. The few nobles and chiefs who are left have lost their powers to keep you safe. The wise Elders who knew the lineages and the history are all dead. The medicine men and women are gone. Hunters and farmers have died, and so have the old people and the children who depended on them for food. There are more dead people than living people left to bury them.

Despite the catastrophes, we survived.

THE HAUDENOSAUNEE CONFEDERACY:
"THE WHOLE HOUSE"

1451 to the present

Indigenous Peoples in the Northeast came together to create one of the world's oldest surviving confederacies. The Mohawk, Oneida, Onondaga, Cayuga, and Seneca of the Haudenosaunee Confederacy were joined by the Tuscarora in 1722. Since then, they have been called the Six Nations. The center of life for the people of the northeastern forests was their hodensote, or longhouse. Haudenosaunee means "the whole house."

Longhouses were large wooden buildings framed with saplings and covered with spruce bark. An average longhouse was 18.3 meters (60 feet) long, 4.9 meters (16 feet) wide, and 4.6 meters (15 feet) high. A long corridor ran the length of the building, dotted by hearths, one for each family connected by blood or marriage. Along the sides were platforms on which families slept together near their hearth.

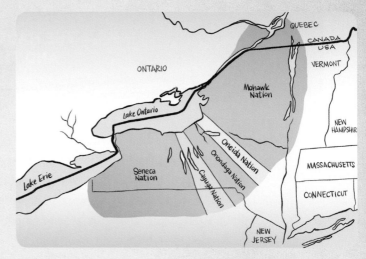

If you were going to live in peace in such close quarters, you had to learn how to get along. Harmony is an important value for all of Haudenosaunee life. The confederacy is modeled on a symbolic longhouse that covers all of the Six Nations, and each nation has its place in it. For example, the Mohawk are known as the "keepers of the eastern door," and the Onondaga are the "keepers of the fire."

A hand-colored woodcut showing longhouses on Manhattan Island before the arrival of Dutch settlers

THE HAUDENOSAUNEE CONFEDERACY AND THE AMERICAN CONSTITUTION

The Europeans who settled on Turtle Island formed colonies. Over time, the members of the colonies decided to join together. They looked at different kinds of confederacies.

The principles of the Great Laws of Peace of the Haudenosaunee Confederacy—peace, justice, and the wisdom of Elders—were an important influence on the framers of the Constitution, the basis of the national government and fundamental law of what would become the United States.

On June 25, 1744, delegates of the Six Nations met with colonists from Maryland, Pennsylvania, and Virginia in Lancaster, Pennsylvania. A member of the Onondaga Nation, Canassatego, suggested to colonists that they form a confederacy. The minutes of that meeting record him urging the colonists to "receive these your brethren with open arms; unite yourselves to them in the covenant chain and be you with them as one body and one soul."

He described how unity and friendship among the members of what was then called the

Iroquois Confederacy (now Haudenosaunee Confederacy) made them all strong. "We are a powerful Confederacy and by your observing the same methods our wise forefathers have taken, you will acquire much strength and power; therefore, whatever befalls, do not fall out with one another."

Benjamin Franklin published an account of the meeting. Seven years later, in 1754, he presented his Plan of the Union. He said that if six Indigenous nations could form a union that had lasted for centuries, surely ten colonies could find a way to work together.

In 1988, the 100th U.S. Congress passed a resolution that recognized the contribution of the Six Nations of the Iroquois Confederacy to the development of the U.S. government.

WHAT IS **WAMPUM?**

Quahog clams are found in the waters along the east coast. People cut tube-shaped beads from the black, purple, and white interior surface of their shells. Quahog beads are also called wampum and were prized for adorning clothing and as a form of money.

Wampum belts have spiritual and political meaning. Wampum belts and wampum strings have been a way to conduct politics or treaty negotiations between neighbors. Wampum can act as an invitation to meet and negotiate. The colors and the number of strings tell what the meeting will be about. At the end of the strings is a wooden stick with notches. Every day a notch is cut off, until none are left. This marks the meeting date. Most important, wampum strings can be used to make a record of agreements.

To this day, people who have the training to make and read wampum belts are our highly respected oral historians and storytellers.

THE REAL POCAHONTAS AND THE WAHUNSUNACOCK (POWHATAN) CONFEDERACY

1595 to 1617

The first federation to form after the English came to the green, rolling hills of what is now Virginia was called the Powhatan Confederacy. The people there called their homeland Tsenacomoco. As a defense against settlers from England, a man named Wahunsunacock (the English called him Powhatan) brought together people from thirty different settlements, each

An engraving from 1624 showing Powhatan in the royal wigwam, wearing a crown of feathers

33

with its own chief or werowance. Wahunsunacock had 14,000 to 21,000 followers. He made himself the mamanatowick, or chief of chiefs.

The colony of Jamestown was turning out to be a disaster for English settlers. They were hungry and sick. They would have died except that Wahunsunacock's people provided them with food. He was happy to offer whatever help he could, because he hoped that the English would become the thirty-first chiefdom, and he would be their leader.

One of Wahunsunacock's many daughters was named Amonute but was often called Pocahontas ("mischievous one"). She had always been curious about the English people at Jamestown. She was funny and good-natured and soon became a lively favorite with the English.

John Smith was one of the men governing Jamestown. In 1624 he wrote about his experience as Wahunsunacock's prisoner. According to Smith, he was about to be clubbed to death in a ritual execution ceremony. Pocahantas, who was then 11 or 12, intervened to save his life.

Smith had not been in danger at all. There was an Indigenous ceremony in which young men went through a mock execution with a sponsor "saving" the "victim." Pocahontas "saved" John Smith as part of this "sparing the life" ritual, which was a step in his being accepted by her people.

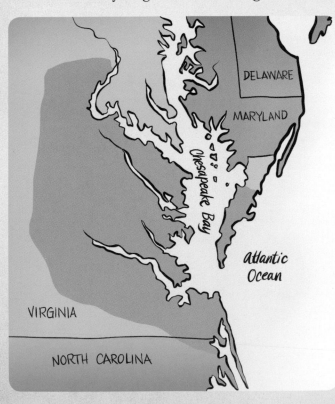

There are countless stories about Pocahontas. Even though some may have been made up, she really was a skillful go-between who constantly tried to help her own people and the English understand each other.

There was plenty of misunderstanding. The English didn't understand the ceremonies of Wahunsunacock's people, and the people didn't understand that the English would never agree to be followers of an Indigenous chief.

Besides, the English were suspicious of Wahunsunacock. Why was he being so generous to them? Those suspicions led to war in 1610.

During the fighting, Pocahontas was captured and taken to live among the English. They changed her name to Lady Rebecca. She married a widower called John Rolfe. That alliance between Wahunsunacock's daughter and the Englishman John Rolfe helped bring about the end of the war in 1614.

To gain support for the Jamestown colony back in England, the Englishman arranged a tour for Rolfe, Pocahontas/Lady Rebecca, and their son, Thomas. "Lady Rebecca" charmed the English, including King James. She and Rolfe were in Gravesend, getting ready to sail home to Virginia, when Pocahontas fell ill. Gravesend was the last place the ship could take fresh water and supplies on board, but before it set out across the Atlantic, Pocahontas died. She was about 21 years old.

Pocahontas had converted to Christianity and she was buried in the cemetery of a church in Gravesend. Her father died a year later.

The conflict between the English and Wahunsunacock's confederacy didn't end in 1614. Two more wars took place, the last one ending in 1646. The English were firmly settled in Virginia, and what they called the Powhatan Confederacy crumbled.

TECUMSEH'S CONFEDERACY:
PANTHER ACROSS THE SKY

March 1768 to October 5, 1813

Tecumseh was a brilliant Shawnee leader whose name means "Panther Across the Sky" or "Shooting Star." He covered thousands of miles on horseback and by canoe to deliver his message: Indigenous Peoples, even those who belonged to nations that had been enemies for as long as anyone could remember, would be stronger if they joined together in one confederacy.

Tecumseh was a fine debater who could make his case in several languages, and a courageous, generous leader with a deep sense of justice: once, when he heard that his warriors were killing captives, he rode into the middle of the fight and put a stop to it.

There are dozens of stories about Tecumseh's political savvy. Everyone talked about (and maybe embellished) his meeting with William Henry Harrison in Vincennes, the capital of the new Indiana Territory. Harrison was the territory's leader and would one day be president of the United States. In August 1810, Tecumseh paddled up the Wabash River with eighty canoes and several hundred warriors from different nations to meet with Harrison. This was not a short meeting. Translators had a hard time keeping up with Tecumseh's passionate mix of history and poetry.

Tecumseh argued that Indigenous Peoples had the right to act together to resist the power of the United States. Harrison claimed that the United States was being fair to Indigenous people. Tecumseh called Harrison a liar. The two men ended the evening brandishing a tomahawk and a sword at one another.

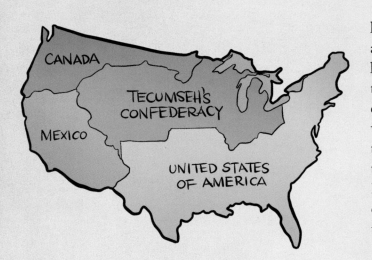

By the next morning, tempers had cooled. Tecumseh apologized, and the two men sat together on a bench to talk things over. As they talked, Tecumseh slid closer and closer to Harrison until Harrison was about to fall off the end of the bench. Harrison finally protested, and Tecumseh laughed. Harrison got the point—he had experienced what was happening to Tecumseh's people.

TECUMSEH
THE ORATOR

Tecumseh was a spellbinding speaker. Someone who heard him describe a major earthquake that had just taken place wrote down his words: "Brothers—the Great Spirit is angry with our enemies; he speaks in thunder, and the earth swallows up villages, and drinks up the Mississippi. The great waters will cover their lowlands; their corn cannot grow; and the Great Spirit will sweep those who escape to the hills from the earth with his terrible breath."

Tecumseh and his brother founded Prophetstown on Tippecanoe Creek as a place where people could live in the old ways. They refused to keep domesticated animals like cows and pigs, and they didn't use any metal and other imported products. Prophetstown lasted until Harrison ordered that the village be ransacked, claiming that the residents had murdered a white settler. Tecumseh had to seek refuge in British territory around the Niagara River.

When the War of 1812 broke out between the Americans and the British, Tecumseh put aside his call for the unity of his people and led his forces to join the British, hoping that the British would support Indigenous Peoples against the United States. After he was killed in the Battle of the Thames in October 1813, his coalition broke apart.

THE FIRST NORTH AMERICAN REFUGEE CAMP

Not surprisingly, many people wanted to get as far away as they could from the invading Spanish (and the English, French, and Dutch who followed them). By the 1670s, some 20,000 people had left their homelands and moved west to small settlements around Green Bay in what is now Michigan. They crowded into what we would today call a refugee camp.

The area around Green Bay quickly became a nightmarish place. Soon there was little game left to hunt, so people were starving. They got sick in the crowded conditions. Yet even around Green Bay, new alliances formed between nations that had once been enemies. People from these nations sealed their new alliances by exchanging gifts, intermarrying, and adopting children from other nations. The new alliances helped them forget old grievances so that everybody had a better chance at survival.

THE MUSCOGEE FEDERATION
AND THE RED STICKS RESISTENCE: *1767*

Dozens of nations flourished on the rich farmland along the Mississippi River. They grew more corn, sunflowers, quinoa, squash, and marsh elder than they could eat themselves. Their farmers produced enough to support people who lived in towns and specialized in making pottery or weaving textiles.

The people built impressive cities around massive earthen mounds. Great ceremonies took place on the flat tops of the mounds in cities such as Cahokia, Ocmulgee, and Moundville, where the nobles and priests could be close to the sky and the gods.

When the invaders came, the people living in the hundreds of small communities nestled in the river valleys and swamps of Alabama,

Tennessee, and parts of Georgia and Florida realized that they had to stand together if they were to defend their land. Together, the Muskogee (Creek), Chickasaw, Choctaw, and Cherokee formed the Muskogee Federation.

The Muskogee Federation brought together very different nations. It was a union held together by their shared customs and myths—and by their having a common enemy: the Europeans.

RABBIT BRINGS FIRE
(TRADITIONAL STORIES FROM MANY NATIONS)

The people came together and said: "How shall we obtain fire?" After much argument, they agreed that Rabbit should try to get fire for the people.

Rabbit went east and crossed the Great Water. When he got to his destination, his hosts gave a dance to welcome him. Rabbit entered the dancing circle. On his head he wore a cap, with four sticks of rosin jutting out of it.

The dancers went closer to the sacred fire in the middle of the circle. Rabbit danced closer and closer. The dancers bowed to the fire, then Rabbit bowed to the fire. He bowed so low that the sticks of rosin in his cap caught on fire and his head was ablaze.

The people were angry. What kind of stranger was this who dared to touch the sacred fire? They charged at Rabbit, but Rabbit could run faster. The people chased him right to the edge of the Great Water, and he swam across it, with his cap in flames on his head. In this way, he brought fire from the east back to his people.

After the United States became a country, a rift split the Muskogee Federation. Some of its members wanted to adopt the white people's ways, including owning African slaves. Others believed in staying with the old traditions.

The traditionalists were convinced that the only way to defend themselves from white invaders was with violence. The old-style warriors were called the Red Sticks, after the wooden weapons they painted red.

Shawnee fighters and Africans who had freed themselves from slavery joined the Red Sticks. With their families, they set up a fortified camp at Tohopeka at the Horseshoe Bend on the Tallapoosa River in present-day Alabama.

In March 1814, General Andrew Jackson's armies attacked the camp. Three hundred of the Red Sticks' wives and children were held hostage to make the men surrender. Of a thousand Red Stick fighters, eight hundred were killed. Jackson lost forty-nine men. Speaking about the Red Sticks, Jackson proudly announced, "They have disappeared from the face of the earth."

The annual Strawberry Ceremony remembering missing and murdered Indigenous women

Gathering of canoes at an event celebrating Canada 150

THE LEADERS of these confederacies understood Eagle's lesson about taking a broad view. Indigenous Peoples put aside ancient differences to work together against the flood of invaers that threatened their way of life. Though they couldn't protect us against many of the troubles to come, we are still finding strength in working together.

Today, Tecumseh's dream of a Pan-Indian nation is embodied in political organizations that work together at a national and international level on issues surrounding the environment, education, and the law. Canada's Assembly of First Nations, the Association on American Indian Affairs, and the International Indian Treaty Council are just three of the groups that have come together to bring about worldwide change to protect the rights of Indigenous people everywhere.

CHAPTER 4

INVADERS' BATTLES

WE WALK THE WAR ROAD
1792 to 1992

We called you the Town-destroyer and to this day, when that name is heard, our women look behind them and turn pale, and our children cling close to the necks of their mothers.

—Seneca chiefs' speech to George Washington, 1790

WALKING THE WAR ROAD

Walking the war road was a time-honored route to esteem and fame on Turtle Island long before the invaders came. Warriors prepared for battle against enemy nations by fasting and making offerings to guardian spirits. When they came home victorious, they were welcomed with shouts of praise, prayers, feasting, sweat lodge ceremonies, and the retelling of war stories to help them return to everyday life. Without those stories and ceremonies, warriors could not ease their minds or rest their souls.

When the invaders brought their conflicts to our shores, a Haudenosaunee woman called Madam Sacho became her own kind of warrior. Despite her obscure origins, her story helps us understand the impact that foreign wars had on the everyday lives of ordinary people.

OTHER PEOPLE'S WARS

The American War of Independence, 1775–1783

The settlers in the American colonies did not want to be ruled by a monarch in England. They waged a war, often called the American Revolution, to overthrow the English and won—founding a new nation, the United States of America. Even before this war started, Indigenous people already knew that the settlers were a bigger threat to them than the government in England. For that reason, northern nations generally sided with the British against the colonists.

Thayendanegea, Mohawk warrior

The War of 1812, 1812–1815

In 1812, the British army was busy fighting the French army in Europe, so the United States decided it was a good time to declare war on Britain. Tecumseh and his troops of Indigenous fighters fought on the British side because they saw that the new United States was a bigger threat to them. One of the most important battles took place near Fort Dearborn in Chicago on August 15, 1812. The Potawatomi were victorious and burned down the fort. Though they won the battle, the war was a disaster for Indigenous Peoples. In response, the U.S. government approved a policy of removing Indigenous people from their new nation. The Potawatomi and other nations were forced to move west.

A detail from the site of Fort Dearborn

THE MYSTERIOUS MADAM SACHO

In their diaries and letters home, soldiers described her in hateful ways: "A very old Squaw." "Wretch." "Hag." Only one wrote anything that even sounds like a name: Madam Sacho.

In the American War of Independence, the Haudenosaunee sided with the British against those who wanted to break away from British rule. On June 15, 1775, George Washington was chosen to be commander in chief of the Continental Army in the American War of Independence against the British. He knew that the Haudenosaunee were strong allies of the enemy. He announced a campaign to make the Haudenosaunee "tremble."

Washington hoped that his soldiers' "attacks [would] distract and terrify the Indians." He added, "It is also to be hoped in their confusion, they may neglect in some places to remove the old men, women and [c]hildren and that these will fall into our hands." Washington argued that American troops would be able to either

The American Civil War, 1861–1865

The Civil War was one of the bloodiest conflicts in American history, pitting Northern states against Southern states that wanted to leave the United States so they could form their own country where they could continue owning slaves. Approximately 20,000 Indigenous soldiers fought in the Civil War on both sides. Even those not involved in the fighting suffered from the violence, the lack of food, and other hardships of war. Whites assumed that the Civil War would sort out whether the North or South would govern the land. In May 1862, President Abraham Lincoln signed the Homestead Act. The government granted its citizens the right to claim up to 65 hectares (160

acres) of land, free of charge, if they would build a home on it and live in it for five years. This completely ignored all the previous land treaties with Indigenous Peoples.

A watercolor from the 1700s showing a Haudenosaunee (Mohawk) woman

defeat the Indian warriors or at the very least "distress . . . them as much as possible, by destroying their villages, and this year's crop." He demanded "the total ruin of their settlements" since the American armies' "future security [would] be . . . in the terror." In all, U.S. troops destroyed forty Haudenosaunee towns and 160,000 bushels of corn, at least a winter's worth of food. Thousands starved to death.

One of the soldiers who served under Major General John Sullivan wrote home about burning the Haudenosaunee villages: "Our Brigade Destroyed about 150 Acres [60 hectares] of the best corn that Ever I saw (some of the Stalks grew 16 feet high [4.9 meters]) besides great Quantities of Beans, Potatoes, Pumpkins, Cucumbers, Squashes & Watermellons." Another soldier recorded that a town "contained nearly fifty houses, in general, very good . . . We found several very fine corn-fields, which afforded the greatest plenty." Still another wrote: "I really feel guilty as I applied the torch to huts that were Homes of Content until we ravagers came spreading desolation everywhere."

In September 1779, Sullivan and his men set a Haudenosaunee village ablaze. They thought it was deserted, so they were shocked to see a white-haired woman standing among the smoldering ashes, looking like a soot-covered ghost.

The soldiers marched her to Sullivan. Washington had ordered that Sullivan take hostages "of every age and sex," but Sullivan surprised his soldiers. He didn't take Madam Sacho hostage. Instead, he gave her good food to eat, though the soldiers' own rations were running low. Maybe his acts of kindness were a way to raise his soldiers' morale. After all, most of them were farmers who hated having to destroy any crops—even those that belonged to the enemy. They especially hated to burn orchards because they knew how many years would pass before new trees could bear fruit. Or maybe Sullivan just didn't have the heart to murder a defenseless old woman (though that seems unlikely considering how many innocent people had been killed already).

You are stirring the pot on your family's cooking fire when somebody shouts, "We must leave!" There is no time for questions. You help the smaller children scramble down from the sleeping platform and lift the baby from her hammock. You reach for the kettle. "Leave it. Leave everything!" your mother cries. This is reassuring. Surely, it means you'll be back. But now you join the others who are rushing out of the longhouse toward the forest. You run, the baby bouncing on your back, past the rustling cornstalks. The corn is ripe under the brilliant autumn sun, but there is no time to pick it. You don't know yet that the corn will never be harvested and that you will never see your home again.

Sullivan and his soldiers believed that frail, old Madam Sacho had been too stubborn to leave her home, or that she had been abandoned by a family who would never return.

Madam Sacho never did explain what she was doing alone in the ruins of the village. Instead, she gave troops detailed information about the Haudenosaunee. She told them in detail how the women had wanted to stay behind in their village.

Was Madam Sacho an old woman whose mind was foggy? Or was she a traitor to her people? The soldiers assumed that she was just a doddering old woman who was betraying her people without realizing what she was doing.

The soldiers didn't know that Haudenosaunee women wield great power. Haudenosaunee matrons were highly respected for their skill in farming, their political smarts, and their wisdom. No matter how old and frail Madam Sacho appeared to them, her children and grandchildren would never have abandoned her.

BELOVED WOMAN

Nanyehi

Nanyehi was born to the Wolf Clan of the Cherokee Nation in what is now Tennessee. She was married to a warrior named Kingfisher. When the Cherokee and Creek battled over land, Nanyehi fought alongside her husband. Kingfisher was killed, but the unstoppable Nanyehi led a charge against the Creek that won the battle for the Cherokee.

To honor her great bravery, the Cherokee named her "Beloved Woman." Her people believed that the Great Spirit spoke through her, so throughout her long life they sought her opinions. She sat on the Council of Chiefs and had power over prisoners and keeping peace.

After Kingfisher died, Nanyehi married again, this time to a British trader named Bryant Ward. She took the name Nancy Ward, learned to speak English, and studied how the British lived. She encouraged her people to adopt British practices she thought would be useful to them. For instance, she realized that game was growing scarce, so she convinced the Cherokee to raise cattle like the British did.

Nanyehi was convinced that getting along was better than violence, so she helped both sides during the American War of Independence. She supported both the colonists and the Cherokee people.

She supported the British because her Cherokee people sided with them against the colonists. After all, the colonists had stolen their lands.

At the same time, she helped the American side by warning white settlers when the Cherokee were about to attack them. When the Cherokee took a white woman named Lydia Bean captive, Nanyehi freed her. (In return, the grateful Bean taught Nanyehi to make butter and cheese.)

Was Nanyehi a traitor to the Cherokee when she warned white settlers? No. She knew that her people were outnumbered and that their best hope was in peaceful relations. She was so committed to peace that in July 1785, she was one of the negotiators of a treaty between the Cherokee and the new United States.

But over the years, she watched as more and more Cherokee land was occupied by whites. As an old woman, she urged her people not to give up any more of their land. It was no use. By 1819, even the land she'd been born on was lost.

Historians now think that Madam Sacho may have done something very brave. It's likely she deliberately stayed behind knowing she could be killed. Perhaps she wanted the soldiers to be kind to future women captives, or she was gathering useful information for the Haudenosaunee, or she was planting false information with the enemy. One soldier described how she sent Sullivan's men on a wild-goose chase: she "likewise told us that a great deal many Squaws and Children were over a hill . . . in consequence of which . . . a Detachment of 3 or 400 Men" went in search. She had deliberately sent them off in pursuit of—nothing.

Many of the Haudenosaunee were able to escape to British-held forts, but Madam Sacho's story ends in a mystery and a tragedy. A few weeks after the soldiers burned her village, they returned. They found the body of a young Indigenous woman, whose name we don't know, lying in the ashes and mud. She had probably either stayed behind to help Madam Sacho or planned to take a message to her people from Madam Sacho. She had been shot by soldiers. We don't know what happened to Madam Sacho.

In 1790, after the war was over, Seneca chiefs addressed a speech to George Washington, by then the first president of the new United States, saying: "When your army entered the Country of the Six Nations, we called you the Town-destroyer and to this day, when that name is heard, our women look behind them and turn pale, and our children cling close to the necks of their mothers."

MODERN WARRIORS IN MODERN WARS

In all the foreign wars that were fought on North American soil, Indigenous people drew on their centuries of experience to pick alliances. However, none of these foreign "allies" would prove to be on their side when it came to protecting Indigenous Peoples' right to own, occupy, and manage their own land.

Nevertheless, Indigenous people have distinguished themselves in the modern military. In the United States, Indigenous men and women serve in the Armed Forces in greater numbers statistically than any other group. Since the Medal of Honor was established in 1862 as the U.S.'s highest military honor, twenty-seven Indigenous Americans have received it.

Gregory "Pappy" Boyington, Medal of Honor recipient

There are more than 1,200 Indigenous Canadians in the Armed Forces from 640 different bands. Many of them come from families that have served proudly for generations. From World War I to the wars in Korea, Vietnam, Iraq, and Afghanistan, more than 500 have lost their lives on foreign battlefields.

Perhaps one reason so many have taken the path of joining the army may be that military service is a way out of the poverty and joblessness that many Indigenous people face. While walking the war road, young men have always found adventure and opportunities to display their bravery. We've cheered them on as they've gone into battle, and we've welcomed them with songs and ceremonies like the sweat lodge when they've returned home. Today, some veterans from all backgrounds find support in these traditions that help them ease their way back into their communities.

CODE
TALKERS

Code talkers were Indigenous soldiers in World War II (1939–1945) who spoke Navajo, Cree, and Comanche. They used their languages to send secret military messages by radio, telephone, and telegraph. The Germans and Japanese did not know any Indigenous languages. To them, the messages were in code—codes they never learned to crack. The code talkers were sworn to keep their work secret, so we are only now learning how important they were.

Corporal Henry Bake, Jr. (left) and Private First Class George H. Kirk (right), Navajo soldiers who served with a Marine Signal Unit in World War II, operate a portable radio set in a clearing they've just hacked in the dense jungle behind the front lines.

CODE TALKERS
── ON THE ──
EUROPEAN FRONT

Charles Tomkins, known as Checker, was a Métis man from Alberta who spoke Cree. In 1941, he and about a hundred other Indigenous soldiers were summoned to the Canadian High Command (Armed Forces headquarters) in London, England. Even their bosses didn't know why they had been asked to go there.

Tomkins learned he was going to become part of the Air Force's Cree Code Talker Program. As code talkers, Checker and five other Cree-speaking men translated vital information about troop movements and supply lines into Cree. The messages were sent all over Europe to where other Cree code talkers translated them back into English for Allied military commanders.

After the war, Tomkins served another twenty-five years in the military. He had been sworn to secrecy about his work as a code talker, and only revealed his role two months before he died in 2003, at the age of eighty-five.

Charles Chibitty was one of thirteen Comanche men who landed in France on D-Day in 1944, the day when Allied forces invaded France using beach landings in Normandy. Chibitty used a coded form of his language to send and receive secrets for the military. On D-Day, during the landings at Utah Beach, he used the Comanche language to direct aircraft and naval gunfire at targets, and informed other Comanche code talkers at higher headquarters of the tactical situation.

Chibitty survived D-Day, though about 209,000 Allied troops did not. At the end of the war, he and his unit were among the first Americans to liberate Paris and to enter Germany.

CODE TALKERS
ON THE
PACIFIC FRONT

Navajo Code Talkers Veterans Memorial in Window Rock, Arizona, the capital of the Navajo Nation

In the Pacific battles, the U.S. military set up two communication networks. One was for basic messages, and the other was for top-secret messages. The top-secret messages were in Navajo. The Americans correctly guessed that their enemies would never be able to crack a Navajo code. The Marines recruited twenty-nine Navajo code talkers to create and memorize a code made up of 211 new Navajo words for military terms.

By the end of the war, 350 people had learned the code. The code was key in almost every major battle in the Pacific.

When the battles were at their fiercest, two-man teams of code talkers worked in small holes dug into the ground, sometimes for twenty-four hours straight, transmitting messages by radio. In one forty-eight-hour period, the code talkers passed an astounding eight hundred messages between officers and generals. The enemy never cracked the code. Thanks to the Navajo code talkers, the Marines were able to take the Japanese island, Iwo Jima, thus winning a key battle in the war.

The program remained top secret until 1968. In 2001, President George W. Bush awarded each of the twenty-nine original Navajo code talkers with the Congressional Gold Medal.

INDIGENOUS PEOPLE know the courage it takes to walk the war road. That's why we've always respected the bravery of our warriors. We honor them with the sweat lodge when they return from battle. This is only one of the ways we've adapted our traditions to modern times. Our ability to adapt to new ways was tested by the flood of changes that came with the invaders.

CHAPTER 5

NEW DAYS

NEW WAYS

1492 to 1892

A significant number of people believe tribal people still live and dress as they did 300 years ago. During my tenure as principal chief of the Cherokee Nation, national news agencies requesting interviews sometimes asked if . . . I would wear traditional tribal clothing for the interview. I doubt they asked the president of the United States to dress like a pilgrim for an interview.

—Wilma Mankiller (1945–2010)

CHANGING WAYS

From the beginning, life on Turtle Island was always changing. We know that willingness to change and adapt are important tools of survival. When my people came across new objects or foods or ideas that they liked, they adopted them. The Old North Trail was a pathway for trading ideas as much as it was for trading goods.

For many Indigenous Peoples along the northeastern shores of the Atlantic, the first time they met Europeans was as traders. Along with guns and diseases, Europeans brought new goods and ideas to our shores. We chose the ones that we liked and made them our own. Woven cloth and horses were two of them.

WEAVING THE WORLD TOGETHER

Around the time the Spanish explorers were landing thousands of miles south in the Caribbean, other Spanish, English, French, and Portuguese fishermen were sailing to the Grand Banks of Newfoundland to fish for cod. Some came ashore at Tadoussac in Quebec on the St. Lawrence River to gather wood for stands on which to dry their catch.

Tadoussac was where as many as 20,000 Montagnais, Wolastoqiyik, and Mi'kmaq people gathered every summer to fish and trade. The exchanges between the fishermen and the Indigenous were just the beginning of a lively trade.

The Indigenous people had furs, and the Europeans wanted them. Furs, especially beaver, were the rage in Europe for hats and clothing. Since beaver pelts could be exchanged for any item the French trading partners had, one Cree chief stated, *"Le castor fait tout"* (The beaver makes everything).

In exchange, Indigenous people were interested in the objects that had just started being mass-produced in Europe—metal knives, pots and kettles, beads, and especially guns. Most of all, they wanted European cloth.

Cloth is far easier to sew than animal hides, and the steel needles used for cloth last longer than traditional bone needles. Most important, the bolts of wool and cotton fabric appealed to Indigenous people because it came in colors and patterns that couldn't be made with local dyes. The demand for cloth was so great that European factories began to produce specific colors and designs just for North America.

Trade cloth made a dramatic change in the way Indigenous people dressed. Women sewed their families' clothing using European fabrics but in the styles of their own cultures. New garments in bright colors and designs became status symbols.

Mi'kmaq men on the Atlantic coast liked long hunting shirts that fell to their knees, with ties draped around their waists. For women, white shirts tied with silk sashes and worn with red-and-blue leggings became a fashion trend that spread inland from the east coast right across to the northern Great Lakes.

HEALING WAYS

Indigenous people knew about the healing properties of plants. Healers treated the fishermen's aches and pains with medicine, including one made from the inner bark of the willow tree (we use that same ingredient today in aspirin). Because their diets didn't include enough vitamins and essential nutrients, the fishermen often suffered from scurvy and other diseases. The Indigenous people recognized the symptoms of scurvy, so they gave the fishermen fresh meat, corn, and other vegetables, and taught them to brew a tea with the tips of spruce needles. The good diet and tea loaded with naturally occurring vitamin C saved many lives.

Wool blankets were popular in the fur trade because they are warm and much easier to carry than animal hides. Knowing the colors that Indigenous people preferred, the Hudson's Bay Company designed blankets their customers would love. The iconic Hudson's Bay Point Blanket has dark lines woven into the fabric to indicate the size of the blanket. Wool blankets last a long time and they had added value as they could also be repurposed and made into clothing. Receiving a wool blanket as a gift is still a great honor.

HORSE DAYS

In 1519, the Spanish arrived in Mexico with horses in the holds of their ships. For the first time in thousands of years, horses were back in their old homeland. Although the Ice Age animals were smaller, they were the ancestors of the big horses we know today. The few horses that survived the grueling ocean voyage in Spanish ships became a vast herd that brought a new era for many cultures across the continent.

You feel the tremor rise from the ground right up through your feet and body. You see dust first. Out of the dust, monstrous shapes emerge, pounding toward you. There are men growing out of their backs! You want to run, but you can't take your eyes off the amazing sight. Your dog barks frantically.

As the figures draw closer, you recognize one of the men. He's your uncle.

Your father comes out of your tepee and greets your uncle warmly. You can tell he is as curious about the strange beasts as you are.

A beast whinnies. Your dog shies away.

Your uncle laughs. "Don't worry, she's tame."

"What is this? Where is it from?" you ask.

"We walked the Old Trail to Taos. There, we met men from the south, riding these animals. They needed our food, so we traded all the dried buffalo meat and the hides and elk teeth we had. This is a cavala, a horse. Come, pat it."

Your uncle stretches his hand out. You reach up and before you can protest he has swung you onto the animal's back. Frantically, you grab its mane. Your uncle leads the cavala around the camp circle. Everyone has come outside to watch, so though you want to cry, you don't. You've never been so high off the ground before. Soon you adjust to the way the horse moves. You can feel its strength. By the time you get back to your home, you can hardly wait to ride again.

Trade routes from all directions led to Taos Pueblo. The fair in the main plaza buzzed with the calls of traders bartering seeds, silver jewelry, feathers, shells, and pottery. Around 1625, Spaniards brought horses to the trade fair there, and that was where people from the southern Plains got their first horses. They had no name for "horse," so they borrowed the Spanish word, *caballo*, which soon became *cavala*.

Northern Plains people didn't trade directly with the Spanish, but within a hundred years of trading with southern nations, they had horses, too. Northern Plains people had their own explanation for the origin of horses: they were a gift from the spirit world.

With the coming of horses, we soon acquired new stories, traditions, ways of hunting, and ways of making war.

The dog days were a time when people only had dogs to help them pull heavy loads. Life changed drastically when the dog days gave way to the horse days. You could ride farther and faster than you ever could before, but you had fewer choices about where to camp. Horses eat a lot of grass, so you had to camp where there was food and water for your animals. When it got cold, you had to move from the high plains to lowlands where the horses could be sheltered. But you didn't need to find as much firewood: the grasses that horses ate became dung that you could burn for fuel.

HOW DO WE KNOW?

Ice Age Horses

During the last Ice Age, about 14,000 years ago, horses crossed the Bering land bridge to Asia, where they thrived.

When the St. Mary River dam reservoir in southern Alberta was drained for maintenance in 1997, archaeologists made an important discovery. At Wally's Beach on the reservoir, they found fossils of Ice Age animals, as well as imprints of the pathways that led from the prairie down to the river where the animals drank and swam. One of the animals whose fossils were found was an extinct species of horse that had once lived on the North American Plains. Cut marks on the bones showed that the horses found at Wally's Beach had been butchered at the site. We know that early people once hunted these small horses for food. Horses went extinct as the climate warmed and new species, such as the bison, invaded their grazing lands.

HOW HORSES CAME TO THE PEOPLE
(PERMISSION GRANTED BY ELDON YELLOWHORN, BLACKFOOT CONFEDERACY)

Back in the days when Blackfoot people only had dogs to serve them and they made all their tools from stone, there lived a boy who was eager to show that he was grown up. He decided to leave home to seek the help of the spirit beings. He walked out onto the prairie without any destination in mind. After some days, when his water supply was dwindling, he saw a lake in the distance. His delight turned to disappointment when he tasted the water and found that it was brackish, not fit for drinking.

Thirsty and tired, he sat against a boulder and called out to the spirits for help. Soon he fell asleep. In his dream, he heard a clear voice. Water Chief, the spirit of the lake, had heard the young man's plea. "What is troubling you?" he asked.

He listened to the young man's tale of hunger and thirst. Then Water Chief said, "My boy, I can see you have a good heart. Your people will look to you to be a strong chief. I will help you."

Water Chief gestured to the lake. "I am chief of all the animals swimming here. I will give you one of my favorites."

He braided some grasses into a rope. "You must take this rope and walk away from the lake toward the sunrise. You will hear noises, but do not look back until daybreak."

When the boy awoke, he saw the rope and knew that it was a gift from Water Chief. He picked up the rope, and as the dawn broke, he walked toward the east, just as he had been told. He heard strange noises behind him. He was tempted to turn and look, but he remembered Water Chief's words.

Finally, he saw Sun leave his lodge and light the day. Only then did he look behind him. Following him was a strange animal that looked like elk without antlers, but that was as tame as the dogs in his camp. It was a horse. He walked up to the horse with his rope and reached out his hand. It did not shy away. The young man took the animal home, and as Water Chief had promised, he became a great chief. He gave horses their Blackfoot name, elk-dog. Ever since, Blackfoot people have always owned many elk-dogs.

NEW WAYS OF WAR

The federations that bound nations together were no guarantee against war with ancient enemies. Before horses, nations fought against one another in hand-to-hand combat (usually during the summer after the planting season and before harvest) using weapons made from wood, stone, and bone. No one group had an obvious advantage over another.

That balance was upset when some nations got horses and guns. If one nation had horses and guns and an enemy nation did not, war was no longer a battle between equals. Raiders regularly crept into enemy communities to steal horses. Horses gave war parties the power to ride the war road to attack rival villages and to claim trophies to take home.

And when warriors on both sides were on horseback, battles became bloodier than ever before.

SAHKOMAPI

Sahkomapi was a Cree man who became an Elder in the Blackfoot tradition. During the winter of 1783, he taught the mapmaker David Thompson many things. He explained that Blackfoot warriors saw that horses looked like elk but they served humans in the same way dogs did, so they combined the word for elk, *ponoka*, and the word for dog, *imitaa*, to get *ponokaomitaa*, the Blackfoot word for horse.

Elk Tongue (Scout Mobiel) on horseback wearing wartime Kiowa clothing in 1891

THE BATTLE
OF
BELLY RIVER

The Last Great Indian Battle

October 25, 1870

For hundreds of years, the Canadian prairies were home to the Blackfoot Confederacy—made up of the Siksika, Kainai (Blood), and Piikani—and later, the Tsuu T'ina and Gros Ventre—and the Iron Confederacy, an alliance of the Plains Cree, Assiniboine, Plains Ojibwa, Nakoda, and sometimes Métis. The two alliances became enemies over the years and fought many times. Their last battle was the fiercest.

Summer was long gone, and the days were too short to lose their nighttime chill. Winter camps of Blackfoot, Blood, and Piikani clans stretched along Alberta's Oldman River downstream from where it received the water of the Belly River. At the big bend

Oldman River, Lethbridge, Alberta

just upriver from Fort Whoop-Up, where the river turns northward, a camp of Blood and Blackfoot woke to the sound of gunfire and barking dogs.

The Blood and Blackfoot nations had recently lost many people in a smallpox epidemic. The Cree knew their enemies were in a weakened state, so they planned a surprise attack. In the predawn light, Cree warriors swept down from the northeast. Before anyone in the Blood and Blackfoot camp could mount a defense, the battle had already claimed its first victims. Two women who survived the hail of bullets escaped to the river, and they swam across to warn their relatives of the attack.

The Blood and Blackfoot warriors in the camp hurried to get their battle gear and horses ready to fight off the Cree. There were too many Cree for them to fight alone, but the news had spread quickly among the Blood, Blackfoot, and Piikani tepees. They sent their warriors to join the battle.

The Cree were better placed for battle and they had the advantage of surprise, but they soon realized that the Blood and Blackfoot camp they had attacked was only part of a much bigger winter camp that extended for miles. A scout had been keeping watch on the Cree. Around midday, he saw that they were retreating.

As soon as they heard that the Cree were drawing back, the Blood, Blackfoot, and Piikani began their advance. The Cree warriors who stayed behind to fight gave their lives so their companions could escape.

The Cree were quickly overwhelmed. Those who fled to the river and tried to swim across were defenseless. When the day ended, the Blackfoot Confederacy had about forty dead and fifty wounded, and the Cree lost two hundred to three hundred warriors.

The people on the Plains had greater calamities to face. Smallpox and the disappearance of bison were threatening everybody. The bands of both confederacies now shared the prairies. The Battle of Belly River would prove to be the last battle between the nations. A year later, in 1871, the chiefs of the two rival groups met on the shores of the Red Deer River to make a formal peace treaty.

Indian Battle Park lies along the Oldman River as it flows through the city of Lethbridge, Alberta. It commemorates the Cree's disastrous raid into the country of their rivals, in the "last great Indian battle."

COUNTING COUP

In the days before horses, if you could stay beyond the range of your enemy's bows and arrows—the skirmish line—you were safe. A young warrior could show how brave he was by breaking away from the skirmish line to run across the battlefield, strike the enemy with a stick, and race back to his comrades. If he could do that without getting hurt, his feat of daring would earn him the esteem of the Elders. This was called "counting coup."

Horses increased opportunities for warriors to count coup by giving them the ability to ride close enough to strike an enemy with a lance or bow or by hand to humiliate him.

Having witnesses who saw you count coup was important. The more eyewitnesses, the better your reputation. Warriors who showed great courage were rewarded with eagle feathers that were attached to their headdresses or rawhide shields. Each feather told a story. On the prairies, a red feather meant "wounded in combat." A notched one meant "struck blows on the enemy." A feather worn straight up in your headdress showed that you were the first to touch the enemy. If you were the second, the feather was at an angle.

NEW TRADITIONS

Though some of the new traditions didn't have to do with horses directly, they tell us about how much life was changing for us. To this day, the Blackfoot people practice the sweat lodge ceremony and the Ookaan, or Sun Dance, the most sacred Blackfoot ceremony of prayer and sacrifice and renewal. Both began in the dog days and persist to this day. Horses brought about so much social upheaval that old ceremonies were adapted to include the new animals.

Visitors to Glacier National Park in northern Montana can drive along the Going-to-the-Sun Road. Blackfoot people remember this road as a footpath that went west from the Old North Trail just south of the Chief Mountain. Its name commemorates the journey of their hero Scarface (Pawakksski). In Blackfoot geography, this path that Scarface traveled west across the Backbone of the World (the Rocky Mountains) is called Scarface's Road (Pawakksski Ohsokoi).

Members of the Cheyenne nation gather in a Sun Dance lodge before performing the Sun Dance.

This took place a long time ago. There were no horses and there was no Sun Dance, or Ookaan. There lived a young fellow called Scarface (Pawakksski) because of the birthmark on his face. His only family was his sister.

As he grew to be a young man, Scarface fell in love, but he knew his affection would never be returned because of the ugly mark on his face. The ache of loneliness stabbed his heart. His future would be dismal and solitary.

Only Sun, Chief of the Sky World, could change his fate, so Scarface set out on the Old North Trail to seek Sun's aid. All he carried with him was a buffalo horn filled with dried leaves and an ember from his last fire.

When he got near Chief Mountain, he fasted and prayed until he fell asleep. In his dream, Chief of the Mountains showed him kindness and directed him to go west until he reached the Great Water. There he would find the way to Sun's lodge.

When Scarface woke, he searched until he found the path across the Backbone of the World. He walked for many days and endured many hardships. There were many swollen rivers to cross and steep, rocky hills to climb. They schemed to slow his progress.

One morning, he saw that there was only one more ridge left to climb. Before he reached the top, he could smell a different kind of breath. When he saw the Great Water stretch away before him, he knew he was close to his destination.

Scarface ran to the shore, certain he was on the right course, but he still had to find the trail to the sky world. He stopped to rest. As Sun retreated to his lodge, Scarface saw a golden path reflected on the water. He knew it was the trail to the sky world. Carefully, he set his feet on it.

As he walked the golden path, Sun got hotter. Scarface removed the pelt he wore as a cape and held it up as a heat shield. He could scarcely see the path because of Sun's brilliant light.

Suddenly, a voice made him jump. He looked out from under his cape. A young man stood before him. "I am Morningstar. My father is Sun. Come home with me to meet my mother, Moon."

Sun's lodge was not like the tepees sewn together from tanned hides that Scarface was familiar with. It was larger than any lodge he had seen. He could not tell what the covering was made from.

The structure was circular. Logs were set upright in the ground, supporting smaller logs that met along the tops to wall off the outdoors. At the center was one large, branched tree trunk that supported the rafters.

Moon sensed that Scarface had never known his mother, so she was especially kind to him. "Humans rarely get this far into the sky world," she said. "You must be very determined."

Scarface explained that he was journeying to seek help from Sun. Moon agreed to appeal to her husband when he returned to his lodge. Just then, they heard Sun approach. Moon quickly put Scarface behind a screen so he would not burn up or blind his eyes in Sun's bright presence.

As soon as Sun entered his lodge, he knew something was different. He could smell the human.

Morningstar told his father about his new friend. Moon added that she had become fond of the troubled young man.

Sun asked to meet Scarface. Once he had cooled down enough not to injure the young man, he listened as the human related his woes. When Scarface was done, Sun agreed to help him.

He told Scarface to watch carefully as he instructed Morningstar to build a sweat lodge. Sun invited them both to join him in a sweat ceremony. Morningstar was the only boy that Sun knew, so he reshaped Scarface to look like his son, without a scar. When they left the sweat lodge, Sun could not tell the young men apart.

Sun, Moon, and Morningstar enjoyed having Scarface in their family. However, Scarface was starting to feel a longing for his people. He told Sun he wished to be back on earth among them. Sun invited Scarface to remain in the sky world but agreed to send him back to earth. Before Scarface left, Sun gave him the gift of the sweat lodge ceremony.

Then Sun gave Scarface the most important gift of all—the ceremonies that honor Sun and the source of all life—the Ookaan, or Sun Dance. Sun taught Scarface to build lodges for the sacred rituals. Once Scarface had memorized all the songs and rites, Sun told him to go home.

When Scarface returned to his village, his people did not recognize him. He told them who he was and that he had messages from Sun. He showed them how to build sweat lodges and to select the right stones to heat in the fire. He taught the Elders how to perform the honoring ceremonies of the Ookaan, and the people how to build Sun's lodge where the ceremonies would take place.

Scarface lived among the people for a long time, but eventually he longed to be with his adoptive parents and his best friend in the sky world. Sun, Moon, and Morningstar welcomed him back to the sky world, where he lives to this day. You can often see him traveling the sky with Morningstar. You may know him by his Latin name, Jupiter.

INDIAN RELAY

Rodeos are only one way that horses still play a big part in the lives of many people who live on the Plains across North America today. Indigenous cowboys thrill the thousands of fans of the Indian Relay event at rodeos. The Indian Relay is fast, exciting, and dangerous. With only a bridle and their riding skills, contestants ride their horses bareback around a track at speeds topping 65 kilometers (40 miles) an hour. After each lap, the rider leaps from one galloping horse to another—hardly slowing down—until he rounds the track four times. Each team has a "mugger," who must catch the horses after their lap is done, or the team will be disqualified. It is an extraordinary test of courage, skill, and horsemanship.

THE PEOPLE of Turtle Island survived because of our knowledge about the land, education, and medicines, and our ability to adapt. From the beginning, we found ways to live in the frigid north, the swamps of Florida, the prairies, mountains, and deserts. By the time European invaders came, we had centuries of experience in taking new ideas and making them our own. Guns, alcohol, cloth, and horses would all cause dramatic social changes.

We adapted to many kinds of change. But in the next century, we would face changes that almost destroyed us. Almost.

CHAPTER 6

THEY TOOK OUR LAND

VICTORY IS SURVIVAL

1792 to 1992

"Who Found Who?"
—*1492 Who Found Who*, album by Murray Porter (Mohawk singer)

Indigenous people still struggle to understand why so much hatred has been directed toward us. Didn't the explorers who claimed to "discover" our land see our ancestors who were their hosts and their guides? What caused all the violence and brutality? All my ancestors wanted was to live their lives on the land that had been theirs forever. Why wasn't that possible?

The nineteenth century was an especially terrible time for us. White people believed that to build new nations in North America, they had to conquer the Indigenous people who already lived here.

Their excuse was "the doctrine of discovery," the false idea that land was vacant until a white man had seen it. The doctrine of discovery explains why explorers like Alexander Mackenzie and Meriwether Lewis and William Clark became famous for "discovering" land that was "empty." Newspaper editor Horace Greeley wrote in 1859, "These people must die out—there is no help for them. God has given this earth to those who will subdue and cultivate it, and it is vain to struggle against His righteous decree."

White people who claimed they had "discovered" the land thought it was automatically theirs, and that it was therefore acceptable to use violence against anybody who stood in their way.

But the land wasn't empty. We were here.

The fact that any Indigenous people survived the bloodshed of the nineteenth century is a testament to our resilience. With laws and with guns, we were robbed of our land and our lives.

THE TRAIL OF TEARS: REMOVAL BY LAW

It was then the middle of winter, and the cold was unusually severe; the snow had frozen hard upon the ground, and the river was drifting huge masses of ice. The Indians had their families with them; and they brought in their train the wounded and sick, with children newly born, and old men upon the verge of death. They possessed neither tents nor wagons, but only their arms and some provisions . . . No cry, no sob was heard amongst the assembled crowd; all were silent.

—The French writer Alexis de Tocqueville, witness to part of the "removal"

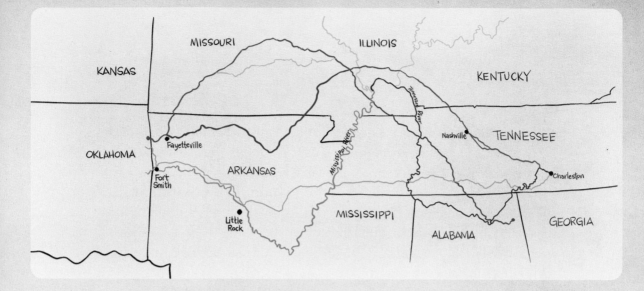

"THE CRUELEST WORK I EVER KNEW"

Wherever the invaders built settlements, Indigenous Peoples lost their land. Between 1492 and 1892, 99 percent of our land was taken from us.

Settlers used their own laws and guns to carry out forced "migrations." Indigenous people were rounded up into what we would now call internment camps, where they fell prey to violent white settlers, disease, and despair. The word *genocide* (the murder of an entire group because of their race or religion) had not been invented yet, but the Indigenous people already knew what it meant.

Since Indigenous leaders had sided with the British against the American colonists, they were considered enemies of the new nation. In 1830, President Andrew Jackson signed a law called the Indian Removal Act, which ordered that the Cherokee, Chickasaw, Choctaw, Creek, and Seminole nations be removed from Georgia to what was called "Indian Territory" west of the Mississippi River.

Senators Daniel Webster and Henry Clay spoke out strongly against the Indian Removal Act. The Reverend Samuel Worcester even went to the Supreme Court to challenge Georgia's attempt to take away Indigenous land titles, and the Supreme Court agreed with him. President Jackson ignored the ruling. He ordered the army to enforce the Removal Act anyway.

The Choctaw were the first to go. There had been around 20,000 Choctaw people before the removal. During the 805 kilometer (500 mile) trek, more than 2,500 Choctaw people died of exposure, starvation, and attacks on them by settlers.

The Cherokee heard what had happened to the Choctaw. Some fled to Canada and to Mexico, but most decided to stay on their lands for as long as they could.

The day they dreaded finally arrived. The journalist James Mooney described the scene when the U.S. Army forced the Cherokee out:

Troops were disposed at various points throughout the Cherokee country, where stockade forts were erected for gathering in and holding the Indians preparatory to removal. From these, squads of troops were sent to search out with rifle and bayonet every small cabin hidden away in the coves or by the sides of mountain streams, to seize and bring in as prisoners all the occupants . . . Families at dinner were startled by the sudden gleam of bayonets . . . [and were] driven with blows and oaths along the weary miles of trail that led to the stockade . . . On turning for one last look . . . they saw their homes in flames.

The Cherokee were rounded up in the summer of 1838 and loaded onto boats that transported them down the Tennessee, Ohio, and Mississippi rivers into Indian Territory, where they were held in prison camps for months.

Then, in the dead of winter, they were forced to walk from the prison camps to what is now northeastern Oklahoma. Of the 16,000 Cherokee who were

This drawing shows the people of a village who have been forced to leave their homes.

REMEMBERING

Even after two hundred years, that awful journey along the "trail where they cried" is an important cultural memory for the Cherokee and other nations affected by the Indian Removal Act. They are working to make sure nobody forgets what took place. The Oklahoma chapter of the Trail of Tears Association accepted the task of marking the graves of survivors with bronze memorials.

—Information provided by the Cherokee Nation Cultural Resource Center

A pathway in the Trail of Tears in Arkansas

force-marched out of their own country, only half survived the ordeal. The Cherokee Nation calls this tragic event the Trail of Tears.

Nearly all the Indigenous nations east of the Mississippi River—about 70,000 people—were torn from their homes and relocated to Indian Territory. One soldier said, "I fought through the Civil War and have seen men shot to pieces and slaughtered by thousands, but the Cherokee removal was the cruelest work I ever knew."

REMOVAL BY FORCE

Across Turtle Island the European invaders took our land from us by force. One massacre after another took place from California to Colorado to the prairies. These are only a few of the massacres that took place, often in the name of "law and order." This was not "law and order." It was murder.

THE CALIFORNIA GOLD RUSH, 1848–1855

When gold was discovered in 1848, thousands of people from all over the world descended on California hungry for gold.

Indigenous People died in the Gold Rush from starvation and from outright murder. The Europeans had brought little food with them, so they lived off the land, destroying the Indigenous Peoples' food sources. Salmon and deer were soon gone. Those who didn't starve were in danger of being murdered. Scalp bounties were offered to Europeans to clear the land of Indigenous people. The population of Indigenous people shrank from about 300,000 to about 15,000.

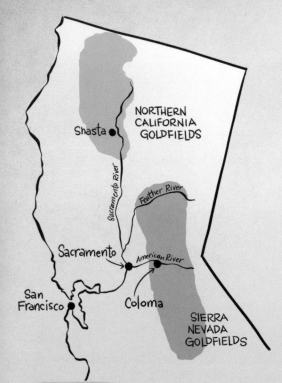

Indigenous and white prospectors pan for gold on the Sacramento River in California.

THE SAND CREEK MASSACRE, 1864

During and after the American Civil War (1861–1865), hundreds of unofficial armed militias were formed to maintain "law and order." In practice, the phrase "law and order" meant all-out war on Indigenous people. The most notorious of the armed militias were the First and Third Regiments of Colorado Volunteers. In 1861, the Colorado Volunteers attacked Cheyenne and Arapaho refugees

camped under a white flag of truce, killing 105 women and children and 28 men. The militia men decorated their hats with their victims' mutilated body parts. These horrific "trophies" were displayed in Denver's Apollo Theater. Everybody knew about the massacre, but nobody did a thing to punish the Volunteers.

"THE FEARING TIME," 1864–1868

Kit Carson's New Mexico militia was as ruthless as the Colorado Volunteers. All through the Civil War, the militia made war on the Navajo, who called it the "fearing time." In March 1864, Carson's troops rounded up eight thousand Navajo civilians and imprisoned them. The Navajo still speak of the Long Walk, the 483 kilometers (300 miles) their ancestors were forced to walk from their land to what amounted to a military internment camp at Bosque Redondo in the southeastern New Mexico desert. At least two thousand died of hunger and disease there. Eventually, the U.S. government realized that keeping them

Navajo prisoners of Kit Carson were forced on the Long Walk in 1864.

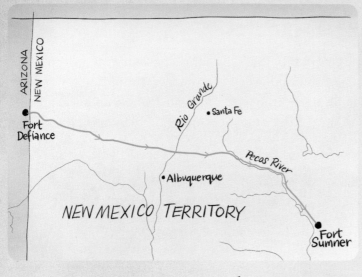

prisoner was too expensive. Under the terms of the Navajo Treaty of 1868—signed by W.T. Sherman and Samuel Tappan for the U. S., and Barboncito, Armijo, and other Navajo chiefs—the people who survived the Long Walk and imprisonment were finally allowed to go back to their homeland in 1868. Today, the Navajo Nation is an Indigenous territory that covers north-western New Mexico, northeastern Arizona, and southeastern Utah. Its 70,000 square kilometers (27,000 square miles) make it the largest reservation in the United States.

MASSACRE ON THE MARIAS RIVER, 1870

Heavy Runner was the chief of a small band of Piikani who made their winter camp along the Marias River in northern Montana. On a January morning in 1870, they had the misfortune of being in the path of U.S. cavalry bent on seeking revenge for the murder of a white settler. Army scouts discovered the Piikani camp before dawn and attacked it as people slept. With their heavily armed force, they murdered nearly two hundred men, women, and children. More died later of exposure and hunger because the cavalry had destroyed the village and the food supply. No one was ever held accountable for this massacre.

MASSACRE AT WOUNDED KNEE, 1890

Wounded Knee was the site of the final battle between the U.S. Army and the Sioux. When Lakota leader Big Foot found out that the U.S. Army was looking for him and his people, he thought the only way to save their lives was to surrender. He was leading his people to surrender to the army in sub-zero weather, when all 350 of them, including 230 women and children, were captured and taken instead to an army camp at Wounded Knee. The army mowed down everyone except a fortunate few who were able to run away. After it was over, 300 bodies were put into mass graves. The bleeding survivors were dragged into a nearby church. It was decorated for Christmas. The banner stretched over the altar read: Peace on Earth and Goodwill to Men.

WOVOKA AND THE GHOST DANCE

Quoitze Ow, or Wovoka, was born in southeast Nevada around 1856. His people, the Paiute, believed he had supernatural powers—that he could make ice fall from the summer sky, light his pipe with the sun, and form icicles in his warm hands. During the solar eclipse of January 1, 1889, Quoitze Ow became ill. During his illness, he had a vision of a new dance; he called it the Ghost Dance. He believed it would perform miracles—the dead would come back to life, the buffalo would be plentiful once more, and the white people would leave Indigenous land. The Ghost Dance soon spread from the Canadian Plains to north Texas. Officials feared and hated the dance, and called the Indigenous people who took part in it "fomenters of disturbance." They set out to make war on "fomenters" such as the Lakota. The Ghost Dance proved to be powerless against bullets fired by U.S. troops.

Today, the Ghost Dance is still practiced by those asking for healing for the earth and for troubles like alcoholism, but it is done so privately.

LAND RUSH: REMOVAL BY GREED

THE CHEROKEE OUTLET

You could read the announcement on posters and in the newspapers: at noon on September 16, 1893, a settler could claim one of the 42,000 parcels of land that used to belong to Indigenous people simply by getting to the spot first. A mob of thousands of white men, women, and children arrived on Cherokee land for the chance to make a claim. "Sooners" who tried to sneak in first were shot dead on the spot by soldiers.

The throngs of settlers during the Oklahoma land rush in 1893

This is how a newspaper reporter for the *Daily Oklahoma State Capital* described the Cherokee Outlet:

Men knocked each other down as they rushed onward. Women shrieked and fell, fainting, only to be trampled and perhaps killed. Men, women and horses were laying [*sic*] all over the prairie.

MOLLIE BURKHART'S STORY: 1920s

By the time the Osage people took refuge on a small reservation in southern Kansas, they had already lost millions of acres of their ancestral land. The new reservation was supposed to be their home forever. Mollie Burkhart had grown up there. But settlers moved into Kansas, so Burkhart and her family were forced to find yet another new place to live.

The Osage wanted to avoid another land rush like the Cherokee Outlet, and they never wanted to move again, so this time they settled on a broken, rocky part of Oklahoma they thought no whites could possibly want. Nobody gave much thought to an agreement that gave the Osage the rights to any minerals on the land. That is, until the day somebody dipped his blanket in a puddle slicked with a shiny liquid and squeezed it out. It was oil. And all the oil in the ground belonged to the Osage!

The United States needed oil to light its lamps and to lubricate the machinery in its factories and on its farms. For a time, in the 1920s, Burkhart and other Osage became the richest people in the world.

The Osage had little experience managing large sums of money, so the government appointed guardians. Some guardians were honest. Others weren't. Millions of Osage dollars disappeared into the guardians' pockets.

Worse still, murderers began stalking the Osage. Burkhart's sister was shot through the head. Her mother and another sister were both poisoned and died. In all, twenty-four members of the Osage died violently and mysteriously. Some were shot dead, while others died when their houses exploded, or in agony from poison. Burkhart was getting sick, too. The local white doctors were giving her what they told her was insulin.

The Osage didn't trust the local sheriffs to investigate properly, so they wrote to the federal government for help. The head of the Bureau of Investigation was J. Edgar Hoover. He wanted the crimes to stop.

When she discovered that she was being given poison instead of medicine, tough Burkhart admitted she was afraid, but she refused to believe that one of the prime suspects was her white husband, Ernest Burkhart. In fact, he was part of a conspiracy by a group of local whites to steal Osage money and was sentenced to life in prison.

Mollie Burkhart was among those Osage who fought to end the guardianship system. In 1931, when she was forty-four years old, she was finally allowed to control her own money. She died in 1937.

The Great Depression and the guardians' thefts took much of the Osage wealth, but today they operate casinos that bring in millions of dollars.

By the time the nineteenth century ended, our population had dwindled to fewer than 300,000. We had suffered genocide by law and by guns. Starvation, too. Settlers had wiped out the buffalo herds on the plains to crush the hunting cultures and to make the land available for farmers. On the west coast, settlers had taken control of important salmon resources and banned Indigenous people from using their customary fishing methods. There's not much difference between a bullet and starvation. Both are killers. Yet we still had to face another kind of genocide. Cultural genocide.

CHAPTER 7

ASSIMILATION

WE RESIST

1500 to 1992

I want to get rid of the Indian problem . . .
Our objective is to continue until there is not a single Indian
in Canada that has not been absorbed into the body politic and
there is no Indian question, and no Indian Department . . .

—Duncan Campbell Scott,
head of Canada's Department of Indian Affairs, 1913–1932

Our land was taken from us by laws, and our lives were lost to disease, starvation, and violence. But there is another way to destroy a people. It can happen more slowly, through assimilation. White people thought that if Indigenous people would only assimilate—in other words, give up their traditional ways (religion, ways of educating children, their families, and even their names) and replace them with white ways—everybody would be better off. Even those who wanted to do good didn't understand that if you want to make someone become like you, it's because you assume you are superior.

Europeans were so convinced that their ways were better than ours that when they first saw the great Mississippian cities like Cahokia, they refused to believe that Indigenous people could build such magnificent structures. Instead, they made up legends about a fabled race of white people they called the Moundbuilders who were killed off by Indigenous people.

Forcing us to assimilate—to be like white people—is a kind of white supremacy. It assumes that their way of life is the normal condition for all people. Assimilation also meant there would be no need to settle land claims or honor treaties. Through it all, we resisted and kept our identities alive.

PRAYER TOWNS: ASSIMILATION BY RELIGION

Beginning with the Spanish in the early 1500s, Europeans have sent missionaries to convert Indigenous people to Christianity.

In 1651, John Eliot, an English Puritan missionary, received 810 hectares (2,000 acres) of land near what is now Boston so that Christian Indians could build an English-style town, complete with clapboard houses and even a pretty, arched footbridge that crossed the river. The town was called Natick. There, Indigenous people could be English.

Soon, all Christian Indigenous people in the area had to live in one

A drawing depicts John Eliot preaching to Indigenous people in the 1600s of four such "prayer towns." Non-Christian Indigenous people were called "strangers," and nobody in the prayer towns was supposed to allow them in their homes. The name of every person in prayer towns was recorded once a year. If you had to leave your town for any reason, you needed a magistrate's certificate proving that you would come back and not forget your new Christian faith. When an English person approached you on the street, you had to lay down any weapons you were carrying and wait while that person looked over your papers. If you broke the rules, you could be fined or flogged.

RESIST: KEEPING THE FAITH

In both Canada and the U.S., Indigenous religious practices like the Sun Dance and the sweat lodge were banned or were impossible to practice because we had lost access to our sacred places through treaties. Possession of certain sacred objects needed for the rituals, like the peyote cactus and eagle feathers and bones, was prohibited.

Traditional Aztec shaman in modern-day Mexico City

Christianity is still a common form of religious observance among some Indigenous people, but many of them also take part in traditional practices. Some Haudenosaunee practice the Longhouse Religion, which is sometimes called Gaiwiio or "Good Word" and combines aspects of Christianity with traditional beliefs. In 1978, the American Indian Religious Freedom Act was passed in the United States, finally making the Indigenous religious ceremonies legal.

In Mexico, where the Spaniards read out the Spanish Requirement for the first time over five hundred years ago, some people now practice a new religion, Mexicayotl ("Essence of the Mexican"), which draws on ancient Aztec philosophy. One of the founders and spiritual leaders, Francisco Jimenez Sanchez, founded the In Kaltonal or "House of the Sun," also called the Native Mexican Church in the 1970s. Since then, Mexicayotl has spread among Mexicans and Mexican Americans. The Native Mexican Church was officially recognized by the government of Mexico in 2007.

"KILL THE INDIAN IN HIM, AND SAVE THE MAN":

ASSIMILATION BY EDUCATION

From the beginning of our history, we have had our own ways of passing on knowledge to new generations through oral tradition, our symbols, our art, and even our writing. Among our ancestors were mathematicians, architects, and astronomers. They designed and built our ancient roads, canals, and great cities. They were traders and military leaders and healers, and historians who remembered our family lineages and our past.

In my tradition, we knew how to read all kinds of images. My ancestors used symbols from their dreams to decorate their tepees. They painted and scratched onto rocks the images that archaeologists call pictographs and petroglyphs. Every nation had its winter count, a tribal history sketched in panels on a buffalo robe using ocher and plant paints. The keeper gave each winter a unique name, and the glyph aided his memory when he talked about it. Warriors captured their war exploits on a buffalo hide that might become a shirt or double as a door.

When writing in the European tradition reached the Plains, the people did not think of it as magical. They recognized it immediately as another way of expressing ideas. The only difference was that it was done with pen and ink on paper instead of paint on hides and rocks.

Pictograph rock art at Seminole Canyon State and Historic Site Park in Texas

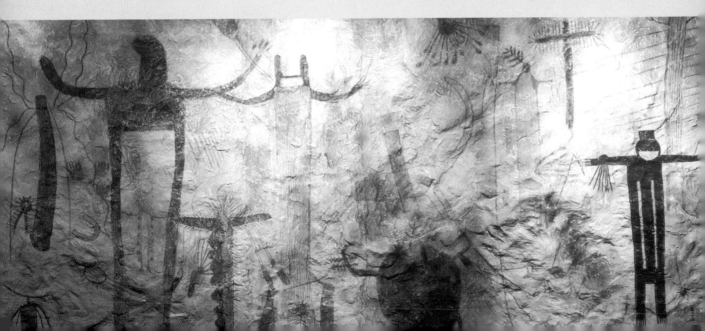

THE LOST SACRED SCROLLS

Anishinaabe people had a form of writing called Wiigwaasabak. To make their hallowed scrolls, first they peeled the bark from a birch tree. They scraped away the dark part of the bark or scratched lines in it to reveal the lighter bark. By contrasting the light and dark shades, they could create the panels and images used by the sacred Midewiwin (the Grand Medicine Society). They used charcoal and red and blue dyes to write on the scrolls. After the Canadian government passed the Indian Act in 1876, many traditional ceremonies were banned and some of the scrolls were lost or destroyed. Other scrolls were stored in special boxes and hidden in secret places in the woods or buried in caves to keep them safe.

In the 1930s, an American anthropologist, Alfred Irving Hallowell, took a bundle of the sacred scrolls to the United States, where they were stored at the Smithsonian Institution in Washington. Some of the scrolls are at least four hundred years old, a priceless record of maps, history, and instructions on how to perform rituals. After seventy years at the Smithsonian, the scrolls were finally returned to the Anishinaabe people.

Europeans didn't recognize our traditional ways of teaching and learning. They thought that they would be helping us assimilate if they took over our education.

In the mid-1600s, Harvard College established an "Indian College" for Indigenous people from New England. It was like a high school at a time when very few people, European or Indigenous, got any higher education. Other similar schools were created by missionaries, but as Indigenous people were forced onto reservations, boarding schools became much more common.

Richard Pratt, founder of the Carlisle Indian Industrial School (the model for residential schools in Canada and the U.S.), was an army officer. He based residential schools on an educational program originally used in a prison for Indigenous people. This is what he said in 1892: "All the Indian there is in the race should be dead. Kill the Indian in him, and save the man."

Students at the Carlisle Indian Industrial School in Pennsylvania in 1884

imagine

>>>>>>>>>>>>>>>>>>>>

You are only seven years old. Your parents cry as they put you on a train with other children. They explain that they have no choice. The train takes you far away, to the largest building you've ever seen. When you get to the school, the matron bathes you in kerosene and shaves your head. Long hair like the people wear at home is forbidden.

You used to live among people who love you, but now you are surrounded by strangers. Your brother and sister are at the school, but you aren't allowed to speak to each other. When one of the teachers beats you, there is nobody to protect you. You forget your own language because you are punished when you don't speak English. You are even given a new name.

Granted, you learn skills, but you begin to forget the skills you learned at home. When you do get to go home, it's hard to fit in because you've been taught to feel ashamed of your traditional life.

Education in boarding schools and residential schools across North America was not unusual in the nineteenth and twentieth centuries. But Indigenous children were *forced* to leave their families and their way of life behind. At school, they'd work in the mornings and attend classes in the afternoon. They'd speak nothing but English. They'd learn skills like sewing and carpentry so they could find jobs—in the white world. As for their peoples' traditional skills—they were not taught.

From 1838 to 1998, nearly 150,000 Indigenous children aged seven to fifteen were forced to leave their homes and sent to one of eighty residential schools in Canada.

In 1973, there were still 60,000 Indigenous children in boarding schools in the U.S. By 2007, most of the 150 schools in the U.S. had been closed, and the number of Native American children in boarding schools was down to 9,500.

RESIST: THE INDIAN RESIDENTIAL SCHOOLS SETTLEMENT AGREEMENT

Nowadays, the remaining residential schools in the U. S. are very different than those in the past. The schools actively recruit Indigenous teachers. Along with reading and writing and math, today's students study the arts (like beading), learn Indigenous history, and take language classes. Traditional activities such as drum circles and story-telling are encouraged rather than punished.

In Canada, former students filed a class action suit against the Government of Canada and the churches that had run the schools. The result was the Indian Residential Schools Settlement Agreement, the largest class action settlement in Canadian history. From 2007 to 2017, $4.7 billion has been paid to residential school survivors.

The Walk for Reconciliation in Ottawa in 2015 aimed to renew relationships among Indigenous Peoples and all Canadians.

Another outcome of the case was the creation of the Truth and Reconciliation Commission of Canada (TRC) to ensure there was a public record of what had happened in the schools. Its final report included-ninety-four "calls to action" for the future, including respect for Indigenous religions and finding ways to reduce the number of children in foster homes. At least 3,200 children died in residential schools, a much higher rate than for other children in Canada. The National Centre for Truth and Reconciliation is trying to locate all their graves.

On June 11, 2008, the prime minister of Canada, Stephen Harper, made a formal apology to the former students, their families, and their communities for the country's role in residential schools.

THE SIXTIES SCOOP:

ASSIMILATION BY ADOPTION

Adoption has always been part of Indigenous life. In the past, defeated warriors, women, or children might be adopted by their captors. Such adoptions were a way to replenish a tribe's numbers when members died in battle. This happened so often that honorary adoptions of youths from other nations were part of peace treaties and friendship ceremonies among nations. It is still a great honor to be adopted into a nation. You can be sure you will be treated as kin.

The Sixties Scoop was a totally different kind of adoption. In Canada in 1951, the provinces became responsible for the welfare of Indigenous children. After centuries of hardship, too many Indigenous people were struggling with poverty, bad health, and addiction. Social workers thought they were doing a good thing when they "scooped" children out of their homes to remove them from these hard conditions.

Most social workers knew little about Indigenous culture. When they saw children eating dried meat and fish and berries, they assumed these traditional, healthy "country foods" would leave them malnourished. They also did not know that customary adoptions and co-parenting arrangements were common, so when they saw children living with people other than their parents, they thought the children were being neglected.

Social workers did not ask the community if they could "scoop" up children. They could decide whether or not to let the band council know. The number of children taken in this manner started small but eventually thousands disappeared. In British Columbia in 1951, only 29 children had been seized. By 1954, that number had grown to 1,466.

Over the years, more than 20,000 Indigenous children in Canada were taken from their homes and placed with white families. Half of them were sent to homes in the United States, and some were even sent as far away as New Zealand.

In good adoptive homes, the parents were warm and loving and believed that they were giving the children the best chance at life. But if they didn't understand Indigenous culture, even the most loving adoptive parents couldn't teach the children about their heritage. Some even thought that they could protect the children from discrimination if they pretended they were Italian or Spanish.

The result? Thousands of children scooped from their homes grew up with no identity and feeling like they didn't belong anywhere. They were not white, yet they had no connections to their first cultures.

RESIST: WE USE THE LAW

Many of the children taken from their homes are now adults, and they are looking for the families they lost during their years away.

Like the survivors of residential schools, survivors of the Sixties Scoop filed their own class action suit against the Canadian government. They won. On October 6, 2017, the Canadian government announced a settlement of $800 million for Sixties Scoop survivors.

Sadly, despite new laws that give local bands the power to take care of child and family services, little has changed. Today, the reasons children are taken from their homes often have to do with neglect, poor housing, and substance abuse, conditions that are linked to poverty. In British Columbia, 51 percent of the children in care are Indigenous, even though Indigenous people make up only 8 percent of the population.

Chief Marcia Brown Martel and several Sixties Scoop survivors attend a news conference in 2017 announcing a compensation package for Indigenous victims of the Sixties Scoop.

WHAT'S YOUR NUMBER?
ASSIMILATION THROUGH NEW NAMES

One of the oddest plans to assimilate people was Project Surname. Names have always meant a lot in Inuit culture. An expectant mother might receive a name from a dream or vision. Somebody who lost a loved one might recognize that person's nature in a new baby. Giving a child a dead person's name was a way to bring a loved one's spirit back to the community. A baby could be given several names until the name that best suited the child became obvious. If a name didn't prove to fit the child's personality or if it seemed to bring bad luck, it was changed.

All this was perfectly clear to every Inuk, but traditional ways of naming baffled missionaries and government officials. Also, they had trouble pronouncing Inuit names, which were often spelled differently on different documents. Since every name was unique and families had no surnames, government agents couldn't keep track of who belonged to which family. Of course, the Inuit themselves had no problem knowing their own families.

First, the government decided to solve its name problem by fingerprinting every Inuk. Missionaries and federal agents protested—fingerprinting was for criminals, not innocent people. The answer? In 1935, a medical officer posted in Pangnirtung (now Nunavut) had a new idea: let's give every Inuk an identification disk and a number! And that's what happened.

Starting in 1944, every Inuk received a burgundy disk made of felt or leather. Along the edge were the words *Eskimo Identification Canada*. There was a crown in the center. An *E* or *W* meant *East* or *West Arctic*. Then there was a

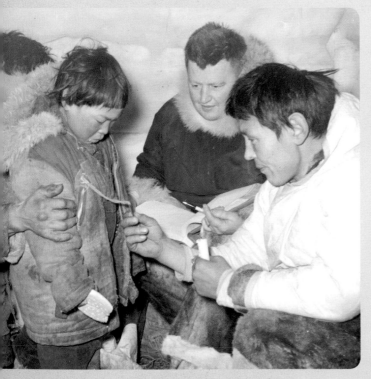

Taking the census in 1950 in in Windy River, Northwest Territories

number representing one of the twelve geographic areas of government authority. Finally, there was a personal identification number to be used for everything "official," from registering births to recording weddings and deaths. The Inuit were expected to have their tags on them all the time—sewn to a jacket or worn as a necklace.

In 1970, the Government of Canada replaced disks with Project Surname. Government officials would show up at your house and help you pick a surname and how you wanted to spell it. The problem was that if you were away when Project Surname bureaucrats came calling, you could come home to a brand-new name.

RESIST: *WE* CHOOSE OUR NAMES

When the Nunavut territory was established on April 1, 1999, the Inuit became the first Indigenous People in the world to get back their territory based on ancient land claims. They wanted to use their customary names for the geography of Nunavut. The town of Frobisher Bay, named after Martin Frobisher, an English explorer of the 1500s, had already changed its name to Iqaluit, which means "many fishes" in Inuktitut. It became the capital of Nunavut on April 19, 1999. Soon, places all over Nunavut went back to their traditional names.

Northern lights in Iqaluit

ABRAHAM "ABE" OKPIK (1929–1997)

One of the translators who helped put Project Surname in place was Abraham Okpik. He grew up in the Mackenzie Delta area of the Northwest Territories, where he hunted, trapped, traveled by dog sled, and built igluit out of snow blocks. Okpik helped to simplify the Inuit writing system and translated some of the first books into Inuktitut. He was the first Inuk to sit on what is now the Legislative Assembly of the Northwest Territories.

In 1974, Okpik served as an interpreter for Judge Thomas Berger during the Mackenzie Valley Pipeline Inquiry, which looked at the impact of a gas pipeline on people, animals, and land. A year later he was one of the people hired by the Canadian Broadcasting Corporation (CBC) to report on the hearings. It was difficult. He had to find a way to describe the vast scale of the project to the Inuit community: "When you talk about trillions, imagine six sandhill cranes and maybe six caribou, and try to count all the feathers and the hair on their body if you have time!"

CENTURIES OF WARFARE, enslavement, and violence foretold a grim future—or rather, no future at all—for my people. By the beginning of the twentieth century, Indigenous Peoples and our ways of life seemed doomed. A hopeless, unrelenting darkness settled upon us. The Indigenous population was so small that white North Americans had no trouble forgetting about us. Indigenous people belonged to the past: there was no room for us in the twentieth century.

Finding hope in a bleak history is our challenge, but knowing our story isn't over might be our first sign.

Young woman holding a small chalk board with her disk number, 6010, at Pond Inlet, Nunavut, in 1945

CHAPTER 8

OUR DAY IS NOT OVER

WE DANCE!

1992 to the twenty-first century

We will dance when our laws command us to dance, we will feast when our hearts desire to feast.

—Chief O'waxalagalis
(Kwagu'ł First Nation, 1886)

ISHI: The "Last Wild Indian"

Most of the man's band had been massacred by settlers and gold-frenzied miners during the California Gold Rush. Then, in 1908, surveyors stumbled on the few surviving remnants of the band. The surveyors stole their furs and arrows and bows, everything the band needed to live through the winter. We know this because they wrote about it proudly. One even posed for a photo in a stolen fur robe. Three years later, in 1911, only one member of the band was still alive. In the traditional way, he singed off his hair in mourning for his relatives.

At the end of summer 1911, the man emerged from the forest near Lassen Peak in Northern California. Starving, he reached Oroville, California. The first white man to see him knocked him over with a stick, but then felt ashamed of himself and helped the stranger sit up. The sheriff didn't know what else to do with the man, so he locked him up in a cell for the insane until the Bureau of Indian Affairs could decide what should happen next.

By this time, many believed that Indigenous people had all vanished or lived in remote reservations, so when word spread about the stranger, the curious townspeople of Oroville rushed to take a look at him. Excited journalists described the stranger as a "Stone Age savage."

One of the people who heard the news was an anthropologist named Alfred Kroeber. Anthropologists were eager to find "Stone Age people" so they could study pure "wild Indians" who remembered the old tribal ways. Kroeber hurried to Oroville. He named the man "Ishi," which means "man" in a local language.

Nobody spoke Ishi's language, so Kroeber got permission to bring him to San Francisco to study him at the university there. Kroeber was thrilled he had found "the most uncivilized man in the world."

For the next four years, Ishi was measured, poked and prodded, and recorded. When he caught pneumonia, he was put in a display case to "protect" him while anthropologists continued studying him.

Newspapers called Ishi the "last wild Indian." Readers devoured stories about how he reacted when he was shown modern inventions like streetcars and airplanes. Every weekend, people visited the university to gawk at him. In all, 24,000 people watched him, fascinated, as he sat quietly making arrows and lighting campfires.

Ishi made over four hundred wax cylinders (an early kind of phonograph record) of his people's stories in the Yahi language. In time, he learned some English and made several good friends at the university. He even took them hunting, but he never wanted to go back to his old Yahi land. Perhaps the memories were too painful.

Eventually, Ishi became the janitor at the museum of the university. One of the displays showed the bows and arrows the surveyors had stolen, and the fur robe.

Ishi lived his last years in a university building in San Francisco. When he was dying of tuberculosis, he made his wishes clear: he didn't want his body cut up after he was dead. But when he died in 1916, although his body was cremated, his brain was removed and shipped to the Smithsonian Institution to be studied.

In 1915, people from all over the world flocked to visit the Panama-Pacific International Exposition in San Francisco. A sculptor named James Earle Fraser showed off the sculpture he had made for the event. It was of an exhausted, dying Indigenous man slumped on his starving horse, the setting sun behind him.

Fraser called the sculpture *The End of the Trail*. It stands in Shaler Park in Waupun, Wisconsin. Some people thought it symbolized the "march of progress." A few white people recognized it as a tragedy. In 1920, an unnamed critic wrote about "the national stupidity that has greedily and cruelly destroyed a race of people possessing imagination, integrity, fidelity, and nobility."

Ishi was one of the exhibits at the Exposition.

Ishi wasn't the last of our people, but it was a close call. During the years when Ishi was being studied, there were fewer than 300,000 Indigenous People on Turtle Island—from what had once been a population of some ten million.

Today, our numbers across Turtle Island are in the millions once again. And we're reclaiming our culture by celebrating our rituals, by seeking justice in law courts, and by making our voices heard at home and in the rest of the world.

RECLAIMING OUR TRADITIONS:
POTLATCH AND THE LAWS THAT COMMAND US TO DANCE

Duncan Campbell Scott, who was one of the people responsible for Canada's residential school system, wrote to agents of the Department of Indian Affairs in 1921: "I . . . direct you to use your utmost endeavours to dissuade the Indians from excessive indulgence in the practice of dancing." He was convinced that dancing and other traditional practices were a waste of time and prevented Indigenous people from abandoning their traditional ways.

THE POTLATCH

One of the main cultural practices among Indigenous people of the northwest coast is the potlatch.

For the people of the Pacific Northwest, the potlatch is a way to celebrate who they are. It's a joyful feast that features ceremonial masks, dancing, singing, and plenty of delicious food. In the old days, the person hosting a potlatch would display stacks of blankets, precious copper, dishes, tools, and foods before handing them out to the guests. Today, the host of a potlatch still gives gifts to all the guests. A community potlatch might be held to announce the end of mourning for a chief who has died or to introduce a new chief. Holding a potlatch is a chance to repay debts, to show respect, and to mark important moments in a person's life. A potlatch is a way to commemorate a funeral, adopt a person into the community, raise a totem pole, or build a new lodge.

On April 19, 1884, the Government of Canada amended the Indian Act to make the potlatch illegal. It stated, "Every Indian or other person who engages in or assists in celebrating the Indian festival known as the 'Potlatch' . . . is guilty of a misdemeanor, and shall be liable to imprisonment."

A traditional potlatch in British Columbia in 1914

That didn't stop anybody. Potlatches were just too important to give up, even if they had to take place in secret, or under the pretense that they were Christmas gift-giving gatherings.

Chief O'waxalagalis of the Kwagu'ł First Nation defied the Indian Act. In 1886, he said:

> We will dance when our laws command us to dance, we will feast when our hearts desire to feast. Do we ask the white man, 'Do as the Indian does'? No, we do not. Why then do you ask us, 'Do as the white man does'? It is a strict law that bids us dance. It is a strict law that bids us distribute our property among our friends and neighbors. It is a good law. Let the white man observe his law; we shall observe ours. And now, if you are come to forbid us to dance, begone; if not, you will be welcome to us.

The ban on potlatches was lifted in 1951. Ever since, the potlatch is proudly celebrated in the open.

RECLAIMING OUR LANGUAGES

There used to be 2,000 or so different languages spoken on Turtle Island. Today there are 148.

Our culture is embedded in language. When a language dies, our stories, traditions, histories, and knowledge suffer. Elders and communities are working with linguists (people who study language) to make sure that those spoken languages don't die out. The Government of Canada passed an Indigenous Languages Act in 2019. There is concern that more languages will fall silent because there are no native speakers. Community Elders play an important role because they are often the only people who can speak the language and help preserve it through transmission. However, modern technology is also useful with language apps that can be downloaded onto smartphones.

We're also finding ways to bring back languages that have disappeared. In Massachusetts, the Mashpee Wampanoag Tribe launched Mukayuhsak Weekuw (the Children's House)—a language-immersion preschool and kindergarten—in

2015 to revive the Wôpanâak language. Working with language experts and Elders, they used historical documents and personal diaries to create a dictionary and a grammar guide. Nobody had spoken Wôpanâak for six generations. Now five hundred children are taking some classes in the language, and several are being taught exclusively in it. You already know some Wôpanâak words yourself: *pumpkin*, *moccasin*, *skunk*, and *Massachusetts*.

RECLAIMING OUR MUSIC: RUMBLE!

In 1907, the U.S. government sent out scientists to record Indigenous songs because they were sure that the music would soon vanish, along with Indigenous people. They were so wrong. Not only has Indigenous music survived, it is also at the root of almost every kind of popular music in North America and around the world: blues, folk, rock, and jazz. Probably nobody has been as influential as Link Wray.

Fred Lincoln Wray Jr. was born poor in North Carolina. Wray's family hid their Shawnee heritage, afraid of prejudice, but you can hear the strong traditional influence in the guitar power chord he invented. Even if you've never heard of Link Wray, if you've ever heard an electric guitar, you have heard the power chord. Every rock guitarist uses it.

Link Wray

In 1958, Link Wray & His Ray Men recorded an instrumental called "Rumble." It was the only instrumental to ever be banned because adults were afraid it would arouse rebellious emotions in teenagers. "Rumble" has influenced every rock record that's followed it and every musician, too. In the documentary *Rumble*, Bob Dylan is quoted as saying that it's the best instrumental ever.

HALLELUJAH...

for the "Red, Black on Blues"
—Pura Fé (Tuscarora Nation), singer

Tina Turner

African and Indigenous people came together in North America and, in many ways, share a history. They had to face slavery and dispossession, and had to struggle for freedom. Together, they have blended to create a rich culture of shared dance, religion, and food. This is especially true in music. The list of musicians who have both African and Indigenous heritage is long: Jimi Hendrix, Duke Ellington, Thelonious Monk, Little Richard, Tina Turner. Charley Patton, known as the first King of the Blues, was Choctaw. Scrapper Blackwell was Cherokee. Pura Fé, who sings "Red, Black on Blues," is Tuscarora.

RECLAIMING OUR ANCESTORS:
BRINGING OUR ELDERS HOME

In the nineteenth century, communities everywhere were building museums to display "curiosities" and artifacts. The race was on to see which museums could display the rarest, oldest, and most colorful artifacts and human remains. Thousands of those artifacts had once belonged to Indigenous people, including their bones.

Coffins carrying Igiugig ancestors make the final journey to their burial ground in Alaska

In the early 1970s, when a road was being built in Iowa, workers found the bones of both white people and Indigenous people. Hai-Mecha Eunka (or Maria Pearson), a Yankton Dakota activist, was angry to learn that the remains of the twenty-six white people had been reburied quickly, while the remains of an Indigenous mother and child had been sent to a lab instead. Hai-Mecha Eunka met with the Iowa state governor (after a lot of lobbying and hard work, and not before she had to wait outside his office in traditional dress to get his attention). She said, "You can give me back my people's bones and you can quit digging them up." She didn't stop with Iowa.

Hai-Mecha Eunka was one of the people who worked toward getting a national law passed in the United States. The Native American Graves Protection and Repatriation Act states that the remains of ancestors belong to their descendants. Museums receiving public funds had to make a list of remains so that they could be returned if the descendants wanted them back. Since the law was passed in November 1990, almost 800,000 funerary objects (items buried with a person) and the remains of 32,000 people have gone home.

In Canada, the Task Force on Museums and First Peoples was formed by the Assembly of First Nations and the Canadian Museums Association in 1988. It recommended that museums work with descendant communities to resolve the questions about the remains of their ancestors. If any Indigenous remains are found, their nation must be told. Human remains can't be kept indefinitely by museums if Indigenous people object.

Groups that deal with international Indigenous rights have also become involved so that the remains of Indigenous people in their countries are treated with respect.

Members of the village of Igiugig perform a traditional Yupik blessing dance following the reburial of twenty-four ancestors.

ON APRIL 12, 2000, Ishi's ashes were returned to Indigenous people in California. They discovered that Ishi's brain was being kept in a glass jar in a basement storage room at the Smithsonian. After years of wrangling over who it should be returned to, Floyd Buckskin (Headman of the Ajumawi Hesugawi band) went to Washington to bring Ishi's brain home and unite it with his ashes. He performed sacred ceremonies and refused to let it out of his sight until he got it back to California.

Floyd Buckskin and a group of Indigenous people went up into the wilderness near Lassen Peak, where Ishi and his people had once lived. To make sure that Ishi's ashes and his brain would be united in burial, Buckskin broke the jar containing the ashes. Inside the jar was a note to Ishi from Kroeber. They didn't read it. They realized it was meant to be private between Ishi and Kroeber, so they buried it with the rest of Ishi's remains.

RECLAIMED: THE LAND IS OURS

Several Chiefs gather in Vancouver after the Supreme Court of Canada ruled in favor of the Tsilhqot'in First Nations in 2014

Indigenous groups across North America are using the courts to reclaim the land that used to be theirs. Tsilhqot'in country lies amid the snow-capped mountains of British Columbia. An important decision by the Supreme Court of Canada in June 2014 granted the Tsilhqot'in people "the right to use and control the land and to reap the benefits flowing from it." The ruling means that Indigenous people in Canada retain an interest in their "unceded" territory, the land that was never signed away through a treaty or conquered by war. The Tsilhqot'in got to work right away. They have created a tribal park and have announced their own plans for mining gold and copper with strict environmental controls.

I AM A MEMBER of the Piikani Nation. Before settlers arrived, the Kainai (Blood), Siksika (Blackfoot), and Piikani formed the Blackfoot Confederacy. Together, these bands occupied a huge swath of the northern Plains stretching east from the Rocky Mountains to the Cypress Hills region of southwestern Saskatchewan, and between the North Saskatchewan River and the Yellowstone River, now south of the Canada-U.S. border.

The Kainai reserve (Blood Indian Reserve) includes over 1,400 square kilometers (540 square miles) of Alberta prairie, making it the largest reserve in Canada. As this book is being written, the Kainai Nation is working to resolve its Big Claim.

Their claim against the government concerns the location of boundaries around their reserve, based on a treaty they signed in 1877. The band claim would expand their reserve by 265 square kilometers (102 square miles).

In July 2018, the Kainai and the Government of Canada signed a memorandum of understanding, to address community concerns and to resolve their land claim fairly.

THE STORY OF KATOYIS (KAINAI) (PERMISSION GRANTED BY ELDON YELLOWHORN, BLACKFOOT CONFEDERACY)

Katoyis (or Blood Clot) was the hero who made the world safe by slaying the monsters that prowled the earth. His most fearsome foe was Windsucker, which inhaled people whole.

Katoyis had a plan when he approached Windsucker and Windsucker swallowed him whole. Once inside Windsucker, he found the people it had consumed. He placed a knife on his head and told them to chant along to his song. He began to jump faster and higher each time until he stabbed Windsucker's heart. With his knife, he sliced open Windsucker's belly to rescue his people. Windsucker's intestines spilled out and became the Belly Buttes of southern Alberta, the traditional home of the Kainai. Katoyis left his people and now lives in the sky world. Today, astronomers call him Mars.

The story of Katoyis is just one piece of evidence in the land claim. A report by the Indian Claims Commission in 2007 wrote about the boundaries: "Within these lands, the Blood Tribe was created, and it is within these lands that the Blood Tribe developed both a practical and a spiritual existence. To the Blood Tribe, the home base is sacred."

THE OLD NORTH TRAIL taught us the importance of communication and trade. Travelers along it brought their trade goods, ceremonies, and knowledge that they shared with us. Our Elders held that knowledge and passed it down to us. Today, whenever we see the familiar landmarks of home, we remember what our country means to us. By reclaiming our ceremonies, our languages, and the remains of our ancestors, we ensure that ceremonies history does not become an exhibit on a museum shelf. It is living and breathing. We are reclaiming our past and making it our future.

CHAPTER 9

THE EAGLE HAS LANDED

UNDERSTANDING THE PAST, SOARING INTO THE FUTURE

FINDING THE PAST

Visiting archaeological sites in North and South America during my career has inspired all kinds of ideas about life in ancient times. Studying archaeology also introduced me to the many Indigenous people whose ancestors built those sites. They enriched my research by leading me to solutions as well as helping me find new questions. Despite our language differences, the details of our historical experiences share many similarities. They always talk about what they have lost since their first contact with the larger world. All say they lost their lands and resources. And they say they also lost their cultures, spirituality, and traditions. Now they fear losing their languages. Their stories of losing things remind me that I chose to study archaeology because it is about finding things. Each artifact we unearth has a story to tell and we follow the clues to find it.

Anyone who studies antiquity must take a long view of history, looking at vast spans of time. When I study my own culture, I consider eras that lasted thousands of years. I think of my earliest ancestors, who saw the glaciers covering North America during the Ice Age and who saw the great meltdown when the climate got warm again. I have only my imagination to help me understand the world they saw based on the clues and artifacts I unearth at archaeological sites. I have come to realize that archaeologists have to be storytellers because that is the best way to discuss the objects, relics, and artifacts we find. They reveal much about people and cultures that once were but are no more.

Archaeologist Eldon Yellowhorn (top left at left), a Navajo dig in Arizona (top right), and a dig in East St. Louis, Illinois (bottom left)

CLUES IN THE GROUND

The documents we find in archives were written by the European settlers who came to our country. Because of this, today we frequently see only their side of history, and it is written only in English. My ancestors had no way to create a written record of their stories when they settled on the Peigan (now Piikani) Indian Reserve in 1880 because the Blackfoot language used the oral tradition. I draw on my training as an archaeologist to examine the things they discarded, such as broken glass, pottery shards, metal nails, and butchered bones. Sometimes I even find buttons and toys carved from wood. These objects provide clues to the kinds of lives my ancestors lived after their hunting culture ended. Their diets had to change when the buffalo disappeared and they could no longer travel to the customary places where they gathered berries and other plant foods. I want to learn about their early days as farmers, when they first started growing their own food. How did they learn to be farmers? What kinds of meals did they eat? Also, they had previously lived only in tepees, so how did they learn to build their cabins?

Archaeologists see the objects they find in the ground as a sort of archive; digging into the earth is the best way to explore this "archive." When we find objects that have passed from living memory, such as a stone spear point, we can often easily determine their functions. However, people did much more than

Piikani Elder Conrad Little Leaf makes a tobacco offering at a dig site at Head-Smashed-In Buffalo Jump (top left), unearthing a hearth in Waterton, Alberta (bottom left), and Kevin Black Plume uses a mobile mapper to record a newly identified archaeological site in Waterton (top right)

just make stone tools. They were mobile and they moved across the landscape in all seasons, which means we find the traces of their activities everywhere. So we have to consider more than just the physical place where we find an object. Today, we can be more precise about where we decide to dig since metal detectors or ground-penetrating radar can help us locate sites where there are significant deposits of objects. Mapping archaeological sites is also more accurate now that we can use drones to record our excavations. However, despite these advances, we sometimes still have to rely on our imaginations to fill in the gaps left by the passage of time, like: What was this object for? Who used it? How was it made?

CLUES IN THE ANCESTORS' STORIES

Oral traditions employ the spoken word for songs, prayers, poetry, storytelling, and preserving history. Repeating memories by word of mouth recounts the exploits of ancestors, making them notable until they may even become known as heroic figures possessing supernatural powers. Families always pass down their oral narratives from one generation to the next. These stories may contain details about military service, heroic actions, or new discoveries. They may remain as stories told at family gatherings until one day someone writes them down. Then they become part of recorded history while they persist as oral narratives.

Indigenous storyteller T'uy't'tanat Cease Wyss was the storyteller-in-residence at the Vancouver Public Library in 2018.

Archaeoastronomy is the study of how ancient people interpreted and practiced astronomy, and what role it played in their cultures. It often includes investigating star lore—that is, stories and myths involving stars and the sky. Therefore, when I study the stories my Piikani ancestors told, I consider the knowledge of their sky watchers to interpret some of the narratives from long ago. Although at that time they thought the earth was flat, just like the sky country, their observations of the moon inspired them to create a lunar calendar. By giving each moon a name, such as the "berry-ripening moon," they could better organize and plan their seasonal travels. In winter, they used their accounts about the star people who moved across the sky as a way of keeping time after sunset during the long nights. Ancient peoples used oral narratives to help them figure out the nature of things and to make sense of the world.

An Indigenous storyteller illustrates the history and art of storytelling to visitors.

Garry Sault, a storyteller with the Indigenous nation the Mississaugas of New Credit, celebrates the 200th anniversary of the Battle of York in Toronto in 2013.

CLUES IN ANTHROPOLOGY

As a member of the Squamish Nation, archaeologist Rudy Reimer's research focuses on his home territory and the surrounding areas of the Salish Sea.

Bertha Pallan was the first American Indigenous female archaeologist of Abenaki and Seneca descent.

Anthropology was a young discipline in 1892 when everyone was talking about the "vanishing race" (us!) in North America. Anthropologists back then thought they were in a contest against time—they feared we would soon be extinct. Their mission became a collecting frenzy to fill museums with as many examples of Indigenous cultures as possible. They amassed artworks, wrote down oral narratives, and collected songs on early recording devices. Movies were also used to preserve information and allow for later study of the Indigenous Peoples who were thought to soon disappear. When motion pictures (movies) were first invented, they were silent and in black-and-white, such as *In the Land of the War Canoes* (the original 1914 version known by the title *In the Land of the Head Hunters*), by Edward Curtis. Another example is the documentary *Nanook of the North* (1922), by Robert Flaherty.

Despite those grim predictions, Indigenous people survived and their numbers grew so that they are now very much a part of the modern world. Today, we are the ones studying and writing our own history. We are the anthropologists and archaeologists researching our own cultures. We have been discovering that the official accounts of the past, written from a foreign perspective, are biased against us. We finally have the chance to tell our side of the story.

CLUES IN HISTORY

By studying history, we have learned that the story of Christopher Columbus discovering a "new world" is false. History taught us that he claimed the right to enslave the Indigenous people he met by spreading untruths about their spiritual beliefs. We learned that his superiors, who sponsored

A child wearing traditional clothing plays the drum in Victoria, British Columbia.

his voyage, used these falsehoods to make claims to the lands Columbus said he had discovered.

Since Columbus wrote words on paper to express his mostly imaginary vision of the "new world," his fiction was understood as factual history by those who followed him. Thereafter, discovering new lands, claiming their riches, and saving "lost" souls justified centuries of warfare waged against Indigenous Peoples. We cannot know the future, but we know we will not allow it to be like the past.

A family participates in the 40th Annual Thunderbird American Indian Powwow in New York in 2018.

We look to our past experiences to guide our actions when we encounter problems. However, a personal history is the lifespan of only that person. A community exists over the lifespan of many generations of its citizens, so its history accumulates more stories as the years pass.

Everyone is curious about ancestry and ancestors. We want to know where we came from so we can use that knowledge to build our identities. We rely on the family lore we hear from our parents to fill in some of the blank spaces in our perception of who we are. Perhaps the first lesson we learn from studying history is that it has no end. Just as the eagle sees more of the world from on high, the further we look into the past, the more we realize that the world and all its peoples have their own stories to tell.

CLUES FROM OUR ELDERS

Some historians examine old books, letters, and journals to explain modern conditions or to search for lessons that can guide us in the present and future. Usually, oral history is a starting point: we might approach our older relatives and ask them to share their memories. Perhaps we want to know how young people filled their time without computers, television, or electronic devices. We recognize Elders as knowledge keepers because we have much to learn from their life experiences. They contribute lessons and advice that younger folk can use to guide their plans for the future.

Deb St. Amant (Bezhig Waabshke Ma'iingan Gewetigaabo), Elder-in-Residence at Queen's University in Kingston, Ontario

Tlingit/Haida master carver Nathan Jackson carves a traditional mask in Saxman, Alaska.

Elder Noel Starblanket, who died in April 2019, was an Elder-in-Residence at the University of Regina in Saskatchewan.

Elders represent our closest connection to our ancestors. They carry personal memories of people and relatives who died before we were born. My Piikani Elders practice the ceremonies and rituals of the Sun Dance, or Ookaan, which is part of our culture and gives spiritual guidance to our people. Elders may be retired, but they may also still be working—as teachers or artists or police officers. Now that many Indigenous people live in cities, Elders might be found in friendship centers, prisons, and schools. Universities sometimes have Elders-in-Residence to offer advice or companionship. Public libraries sometimes invite Elders to be storytellers. Museums host Elders who demonstrate traditional skills such as weaving. We look to Elders for their advice and leadership because they have gained their wisdom through age and experience, and we recognize the value of that. Elders are often the links to the spiritual customs of their people and so they are called upon to offer prayers at the beginning of public ceremonies.

GLORIA CRANMER-WEBSTER,
Kwakwaka'wakw, Alert Bay, British Columbia

Dr. Gloria Cranmer-Webster (left) was named an Officer of the Order of Canada in 2017.

From the time Canada became a country in 1867 until 1950, the Government of Canada wanted all Indigenous people to be Christians like their fellow Canadians. So in 1885, it passed a law to ban their traditional spiritual beliefs, including the potlatch. Dan Cranmer was a hereditary chief among the Kwakwaka'wakw of Alert Bay, British Columbia, when he performed an important duty for his people by hosting a secret potlatch in 1921. Although he tried to be discreet, word got out and the police raided the ceremony. Chief Cranmer and the people who attended were charged with breaking the law and were put on trial. All their masks and regalia from the potlatch were seized and sent away to museums. When Chief Cranmer's youngest daughter, Gloria, was born in 1931, no one could have imagined that she would grow up to be the first Indigenous woman in Canada to become an anthropologist. Beginning in the early 1960s, she helped to track down her people's potlatch masks, rattles, and regalia so they could be returned to their rightful home. Finally, in 1980, the Kwakwaka'wakw succeeded in reclaiming their heritage and they opened the U'mista Cultural Centre in their village of Alert Bay to house their potlatch collection.

ISABELLE KNOCKWOOD,
Mi'kmaq, Indian Brook, Nova Scotia

Isabelle Knockwood is awarded an honorary doctorate in 2013 by Saint Mary's University in Halifax, Nova Scotia.

"Nobody teaches you to be an Elder. You have to want to be one and work at it." Isabelle Knockwood was born in Wolfville, Nova Scotia, in 1931. As a young girl, she was sent to a residential school, where she stayed from 1936 to 1947. While she was there, she and the other students became test subjects in nutritional experiments conducted by the Government of Canada. Some children were purposely undernourished to see the effects it would have on their development. Later, she got married and had a family. She was a community activist who believed that Indigenous people had rights that had to be recognized. After raising her family, she attended university, studying anthropology. As an anthropologist, Knockwood began interviewing the students with whom she had attended residential school. In 1992, she wrote a book about their experiences as test subjects. She received an honorary doctorate from Saint Mary's University in 2012, recognizing her lifetime achievements and community activism.

DR. BEATRICE MEDICINE,
Lakota, Standing Rock Sioux Reservation

Beatrice Medicine had a lifelong commitment to the role of women in Indigenous cultures.

Beatrice Medicine was born on August 1, 1923, on the Standing Rock Sioux Reservation in North Dakota and South Dakota. When she died in December 2005, she was a well-respected anthropologist, author, and activist for the rights of women, children, and minorities. Her lifelong career in education began in 1945, when she graduated from teachers college in South Dakota. She then studied anthropology and sociology to make sense of the world. She wanted to build a plan for living that worked for herself and that others could follow as well. The skills Medicine gained gave her the power and confidence to identify as Sioux and American at the same time and to speak both Lakota and English. Using knowledge that only an insider can know, she began studying her own people and culture as a professional anthropologist. Upon retirement from her professorship at the University of California, Northridge, she returned to her home on the Standing Rock Sioux Reservation and began her last career: as an Elder for her community.

SEEING WHAT THE EAGLE SEES

Eagles hold a special place in Blackfoot mythology because they can fly to the sky country. We believe they carry messages up to Sun and bring Sun's teachings down to us. Studying history is like the view an eagle sees when in flight because the higher it soars, the more it can see, and so it has a clearer perspective. We learn a little bit about the past when we examine small fragments of time, but we can learn much more by studying longer durations. So when we examine historical accounts from centuries ago, we can compare them to what we have learned since then. We can recognize the untruths that were once called history and challenge them with evidence and facts we find from our own research. At the same time, we enrich our story when we discover new sources that add new details. The more we know, the better we can refine and update our understanding of our history, which gives us a stronger sense of ourselves as we prepare to meet our future.

GLOSSARY

anthropology: Anthropology is the study of human societies past and present. It has four branches: linguistics (the study of languages), physical anthropology (the study of the origin and evolution of human beings), social anthropology (the study of cultures), and archaeology (the study of past human life and activities).

band: Today, words such as *nation*, *tribe*, *culture*, *people*, or *band* are often used interchangeably. Anthropologists define *band* as a small group of people, usually related to one another. Bands organized together form a *tribe*. Today, these words have specific meanings for governments. In Canada, a band is the basic unit of reserve government under the Indian Act of 1876. The Indian Act defines a band as a "body of Indians a) for whose use and benefit in common, lands, the legal title to which is vested in Her Majesty, have been set apart." In the United States, tribes form the basic governing system for Native American reservations.

clan: A clan is a group of people united by family and common ancestors. People can trace their membership from either female or male ancestors. Some matrilineal (the mother's side) clans are the Haudenosaunee, Haida, and Tsimshian. Clans are usually named after birds and animals. The clan you belong to can give you certain rights, privileges, property, and a role in ceremonies.

cultural belongings: Cultural belongings represent the labor and artistic expression of ancient people and include objects such as stone and wood carvings, metal jewelry, shell and stone beads, and elk teeth.

inukshuk: *Inukshuk* means "stone in the likeness of a human" in Inuktitut, the language spoken by the Inuit. Inuksuit (plural form of inukshuk) are structures made with stones piled on top of one another. They are icons of northern Canada and a way to communicate. Some were built in a line to help drive caribou to favored river crossings. An inukshuk with no arms or legs may mean that there is a food cache, or good hunting and fishing nearby. It can be a memorial or it can be used to give directions like a signpost.

kiva: A kiva is a large, circular, partially or usually completely underground structure that was used by the Pueblo people in the Southwest for important ceremonies or political gatherings.

oral history: Oral history is a way to pass down the stories of the past by word of mouth. An oral history can be a formal, rehearsed account of the past or it can be informal discussion. Ballads use music and lyrics to tell a story in song. Today, the term can mean recordings of a person recounting past events.

potlatch: *Potlatch* comes from the Chinook word *Patshatl*. A potlatch is a ceremony that's part of the government, cultural, and spiritual life of Indigenous Peoples living on the Northwest Coast and in parts of the Western Subarctic. A person claiming a title or name, or receiving one, hosts a potlatch to secure their position. Accepting the invitation is a public recognition of the claim or name. Gifts are distributed to the guests for attending. Hosting several potlatches allows a chief to redistribute his or her wealth and resources. It is also a way for an individual or the whole community to celebrate and mark important events.

reservation: When the United States made treaties with Native American tribes, tracts of land were set aside for reservations. They represent a distinct level of government, separate from the state in which they are located and based on the principle of original tribal sovereignty. Today, reservations are self-governing tribes that handle their own affairs and create their own laws, which must agree with federal laws. Unfortunately, many reservations deal with social problems such as poverty and overcrowded housing. About 22 percent of the 5.2 million Indigenous people in the U.S. live on tribal land.

reserve: Reserve is a Canadian term used to describe reserved tracts of land for the use and occupation of Indigenous people. Usually, reserve lands are remnants of homelands that were absorbed into Canada when it became a country in 1867. Today, nearly half of the 637,660 Indigenous people registered as Indians live on reserves. Creating reserves is no longer public policy since the Indigenous people settling land claims receive settlement lands. Unlike reserve lands, which are held in trust for bands by the Crown, Indigenous people gain "fee simple" titles over their settlement lands.

royalty: Sometimes called monarchy, this is a system of government in which one person is the ruler, usually a king or queen. The monarch rules a kingdom or an empire. The authority in a royalty system is usually inherited, and many people believe that monarchs get their right to rule from gods, or deities.

tribe: *Tribe* is now often used the same way as *band*, but it usually refers to several bands that are politically connected, often through a council of Elders, with a shared language, religious beliefs, and other aspects of culture. People in a tribe are connected to one another by the things they have in common, such as their history, their homeland, and physical symbols like totems.

tumpline: A tumpline is a sling for carrying a load on one's back with a strap that passes around the forehead.

weir: A fishing weir or fish trap is made of stones, reeds, or wooden posts in a river channel. Salmon must leave the sea and swim into rivers to reach their spawning streams. Where rivers spill into the ocean, stone weirs capture fish as they mill about before swimming upstream to begin spawning.

SELECTED SOURCES

Dickason, Olive Patricia, and William Newbigging. *A Concise History of Canada's First Nations*. Toronto: Oxford University Press, 2010.

Dunbar-Ortiz, Roxanne. *An Indigenous Peoples' History of the United States*. Boston: Beacon Press, 2014.

Ehle, John. *Trail of Tears: The Rise and Fall of the Cherokee Nation*. New York: Anchor Books, 1988.

Ewers, John. *The Horse in Blackfoot Indian Culture: With Comparative Material from Other Western Tribes*. Washington: Smithsonian Institution Press, 1955.

Fagan, Brian M. *The Aztecs*. New York: W.H. Freeman and Company, 1984.

Grann, David. *Killers of the Flower Moon: The Osage Murders and the Birth of the FBI*. New York: Doubleday, 2016.

King, Thomas. *The Inconvenient Indian: A Curious Account of Native People in North America*. Toronto: Penguin, 2012.

Lethbridge, Dorothy. "War Paint & Regalia: Canadian Indian Relay Racing." *Canadian Cowboy Country Magazine* (June 6, 2018).

Mann, Charles C. *1491: New Revelations of the Americas Before Columbus*. New York: Vintage, 2011.

Mann, Charles C. *Discovering the New World Columbus Created*. New York: Vintage, 2011.

Page, Jake. *In the Hands of the Great Spirit: The 20,000-Year History of American Indians*. New York: Free Press, 2003.

Resendéz, Andrés. *The Other Slavery: The Uncovered Story of Indian Enslavement in America*. New York: Mariner Books, 2016.

Roberts, David. *The Pueblo Revolt: The Secret Rebellion that Drove the Spaniards Out of the Southwest*. New York: Simon & Schuster Paperbacks, 2004.

Sleeper-Smith, Susan, Juliana Barr, Jean M. O'Brien, Nancy Shoemaker, and Scott Manning Stevens, eds. *Why You Can't Teach United States History without American Indians*. Chapel Hill, North Carolina: University of North Carolina Press, 2015.

Thompson, M. Terry, and Steven M. Egesdal, eds. *Salish Myths and Legends*. Lincoln, Nebraska: University of Nebraska Press, 2008.

Wilson, James. *The Earth Shall Weep: A History of Native America*. London: Picador, 1988.

Winegard, Timothy C. *For King and Kanata: Canadian Indians and the First World War*. Winnipeg: University of Manitoba Press, 2012.

Wissler, Clark, and David Duvall. *Mythology of the Blackfoot Indians*. Lincoln, Nebraska: Bison Books, 2007.

Websites:

Canadian Museum of History, www.historymuseum.ca

Museo Nacional de Antropología (National Museum of Anthropology), www.mna.inah.gob.mx

National Museum of the American Indian, Smithsonian Institution, www.nmai.si.ed

IMAGE CREDITS

COVER: (landscape) Pgiam / iStock / Getty Images; (sky) chuttersnap / Unsplash; (eagle) KenCanning / iStock / Getty Images.

DESIGN ELEMENTS: (decorative borders) latynina / Shutterstock; (night sky) Photo by Jamison McAndie / Unsplash; (forest) Jamison McAndie / Unsplash; (desert) Patrick Hendry / Unsplash; (northern lights) Photo by Federico Bottos / Unsplash.

4–5 Michael Benz / Unsplash; 5 (top) Vladimir Kogan Michael / Shutterstock; (bottom) Michael Benz / Unsplash; 6 (totem) zensu / iStock / Getty Images; (campfire) solarseven / iStock / Getty Images; 7 Library of Congress, Prints and Photographs Division, Edward S. Curtis Collection, LC-USZ62-105498; 8 University of Washington Libraries, Special Collections, NA3960; 9 North Wind Picture Archives; 10 markrhiggins / iStock / Getty Images.

CHAPTER 1: 11 North Wind Picture Archives / Alamy Stock Photo; 12 Michael Rosskothen / Shutterstock; 13 (top) Ivy Close Images / Alamy Stock; (bottom) Library and Archives Canada, Acc. No. R9266-550 Peter Winkworth Collection of Canadiana; 14 (top) Courtesy of Eldon Yellowhorn; (bottom) imageBROKER / Alamy; 15 Library and Archives Canada, Acc. No. 1988-250-11; 16 (top) john t. fowler / Alamy Stock; (bottom) Courtesy of Eldon Yellowhorn; 17 (top) *Viking Shaman with Rune Sticks*, by Abraham Anghik Ruben. Photo © Kipling Gallery; (bottom) Galyna Andrushko / Shutterstock; 18 Peter Hermes Furian / Shutterstock.

CHAPTER 2: 19 Heritage Image Partnership Ltd / Alamy Stock Photo; 20 (top) Asmus Koefoed / Shutterstock; (bottom) duncan1890 / iStockphoto; 21 (top) North Wind Picture Archives / Alamy Stock Photo; (bottom) *King Ferdinand II* (1452–1516) by Michael Sittow (1469–1525), oil on panel, Kunsthistorisches Museum, GG_830; 22 Eduardo Estellez / Shutterstock; 23 (top) Ian Dyball / Shutterstock; (bottom) Taos Pueblo, by Karol M., CC-BY-2.0; 25 Carol Ann Mossa / Shutterstock; 27 (top) Library of Congress, Prints & Photographs Division, LC-DIG-ggbain-14062; (bottom) AP Photo/Felicia Fonseca; 28 Depiction of Toypurina from the mural "Art Heals" (2008), created by Raul González, Ricardo Estrada, and Joseph "Nuke" Montalvo, 60' x 20', Los Angeles, CA, Photo by Jacqueline M. Hidalgo.

CHAPTER 3: 29 Library of Congress, Prints & Photographs Division, LC-DIG-pga-10838; 31 North Wind Picture Archives; 32 North Wind Picture Archives / Alamy Stock Photo; 33 (top) Wampum Wrist Ornament, 18th Century, Native American Collection, Peabody Museum, Harvard University; (bottom) Library of Congress, Prints & Photographs Division, LC-USZ62-73206; 35 Folio 28: Augsburger Wunderzeichenbuch, c.1550; 36 North Wind Picture Archives; 37 Mark Baldwin / Shutterstock; 38 National Park Service / U.S. Department of the Interior; 39 *Rabbit*, ink and lithography, by Donald Chrétien, www.donaldchretien.com; 40 (left) arindambanerjee / Shutterstock; (right) Larisa Sviridova / iStock / Getty Images.

CHAPTER 4: 41 TORWAISTUDIO / Shutterstock; 42 (left) Library of Congress, Prints & Photographs Division, LC-DIG-pga-07585; (right) PhilAugustavo / iStock / Getty Images; 43 Library of Congress, Prints & Photographs Division, LC-DIG-pga-01888; 44-45 hauged / iStock / Getty Images; 44 De Agostini Picture Library / G. Dagli Orti / Bridgeman Images; 45 North Wind Picture Archives; 46 Historic Images / Alamy Stock Photo; 47 Department of Defense. Department of the Navy. U.S. Marine Corps / The U.S. National Archives and Records Administration (NARA); 48 Department of Defense. Department of the Navy / The U.S. National Archives and Records Administration (NARA); 49 The Canadian Press Images / Calgary Herald; 50 Jody Neice / Alamy Stock Photo.

INDEX